A SHORE THING

SCOTTY T

**SIMON &
SCHUSTER**

London · New York · Sydney · Toronto · New Delhi

A CBS COMPANY

First published in Great Britain by Simon & Schuster UK Ltd, 2016
A CBS COMPANY

3 5 7 9 10 8 6 4 2

Simon & Schuster UK Ltd
1st Floor
222 Gray's Inn Road
London WC1X 8HB

www.simonandschuster.co.uk
www.simonandschuster.com.au
www.simonandschuster.co.in

Simon & Schuster Australia, Sydney
Simon & Schuster India, New Delhi

The author and publishers have made all reasonable efforts
to contact copyright-holders for permission, and apologise
for any omissions or errors in the form of credits given.
Corrections may be made to future printings.

A CIP catalogue record for this book
is available from the British Library

Hardback ISBN: 978-1-4711-5952-7
Trade Paperback ISBN: 978-1-4711-6181-0
eBook ISBN: 978-1-4711-5953-4

Typeset in the UK by M Rules
Printed and bound by CPI Group (UK) Ltd, Croydon, CR0 4YY

A SHORE THING

CONTENTS

Prologue

'And the winner of *Celebrity Big Brother* 2016 is . . .'

And then there were two.

After almost a month trapped in that *Celebrity Big Brother* house, I was finally about to find out who the viewers had been voting for as their winner of the latest series.

Was it going to be me, *Geordie Shore*'s full-on shagmeister Scotty T, or was it going to be that ex-*Hollyoaks* bird Stephanie Davis who'd spent the past few weeks cheating on her lad with me fellow housemate Jeremy McConnell? Why I nah who I'd pick!

Anyways, we were just about to find out . . . As I waited for that norty lass Emma Willis to put us out of our misery, I couldn't help feeling a little bit emotional about how far I'd come. As far as most people were concerned I was just some fanny-hungry lad from that filthy MTV reality show when I entered the *CBB* house. But over the course of me stay I think I'd shown a different side of me and I was hoping the public had seen that too. Yeah, I'd necked on a bit, flashed me arse a few times and waved me choppa about the place, but it's not like I'd got so mortal that I ended up banging someone senseless in the house. Not saying it didn't cross me mind, like, but it was different at least!

I wasn't only worried about what the public thought of me. I wanted to make sure that the family and friends and a special loved one I'd left behind were proud of me and pleased to finally see the Scott Timlin that *they* knew on their telly for the very first time.

Introduction

Welcome to Me Book!

Oi oi party crew, thanks for buying me book, like! I hope you enjoy it, cos first of all, it's ALL about me and second of all, it's propa radge!

I nah you're probably thinking to yourself, 'here man, he's only 28 him, what's he got to talk about?' Well, I tell you what, I've got loads me! If you like what you see on *Geordie Shore*, then you're gunna fucking love this book.

You see, the Scotty T you know from the telly is just the tip of the iceberg. I'm not putting it on, I'm not acting up, I'm actually even worse in real life, even if I did try to change people's opinions of me in *Celebrity Big Brother*. What you see on the show is me toning it down! Cos as you'll find out, I've lived me life to the absolute max! So get ready for the ride of your life over the next few hundred pages.

So, what can you look forward to from this book of mine, I hear you thinking? Well, what do you *expect* from Scotty T, man? There's gunna be shagging, kick-offs and getting propa smashed. There's gunna be romance, heartache and threesomes . . . oi oi . . . not to mention a whole load of shitting, pissing and whiteying. There's a load of pissed-up stories of bucking and being a daft shite, having people's lives and getting in bother with the police! You name it, I've done it. Except shagged a fella . . . NEE JOY in that, like!

In fact, before we go any further, I think I need to flash up one of these:

THIS BOOK CONTAINS WICKED STRONG LANGUAGE, ANY AMOUNTS OF SEXUAL SCENES AND REFERENCES FROM THE OUTSET AND THROUGHOUT. BUZZING!!

So don't say I haven't warned you.

If you haven't seen *Geordie Shore* – then why not, like? It's fucking class, man! It's like *Friends*, only imagine all of them getting tanked up on drink and shagging the arses off each other. So I suggest if you carry on reading, you do with extra caution cos I don't wanna be causing any riots!

And to those of you who picked this book up thinking to yourself 'wewwwww, is that Channing Tatum' (cos it happens a LOT!), nah, it's not him, SOZ, but I'm telling you now I might not be him but I'm still lush and definitely have better banter, so stick with me, cos you're in for a pure frisk.

Me name is Scott Timlin. I'm a Newcastle-born lad who got famous on *Geordie Shore*, MTV's show about a bunch of lads and lasses living in a swanky apartment doing what lads and lasses do – i.e. banging and getting smashed. So, as of late 2016, there have been 13 series since it started back in 2011 and it's not only given MTV its fair share of outrageous headlines, but also its highest ratings in the UK. And it's been a massive hit around the world, especially Down Under!

But *Geordie Shore* isn't all I've done. You may also know me from *Ex on the Beach*, a fun and filthy beach-based reality show designed to stitch you clean up with your exes. Lads and lasses will spend a couple of weeks partying with each before the show decides to launch in your ex bird or lad from the past – what a LIBERTY! I also spent a month or so hanging out with Kim Kardashian's pal Jonathan Ceban, David Gest and Darren Day on *Celebrity Big Brother* in January 2016.

In fact, I wasn't just in it, I fucking won the thing. What's the world coming to, eh? And that's not all. I've also dipped me wick into the world of soaps and cameo'd on the Aussie soap *Neighbours*, in which, ermmm, I played meself. That's not even it. I've even been in a Basshunter music video, man. Was wicked!

The Scotty T you know from the telly is just the tip of the iceberg.

Anyways, as you can see, I've been a bit of a TV slut, which I will tell you more about throughout this book.

But, before I carry on and tell you about me life, I just wanna say, this isn't going to be your typical celebrity autobiography. From what I hear, a lot of them are pure boring, banging on about stuff that nee one's even arsed about. Not that I've ever actually read one meself, in fact I dunno if I can even read! I've always been too busy thinking about going out with me pals or grafting a lass than finding the time to sit down and actually read a book, sack that!

I've got a problem concentrating cos I've had ADHD all me life, which means I can't sit still for longer than five minutes without getting sidetracked. I find it hard to focus on one thing at a time and I'm not very good at remembering stuff either. So you'll have to bear with me if I fuck up a few details here and there. I get bored too easily and me mind will just wander off and focus on something else. (So, where we off tonight . . . ?)

Er, soz about that, erm, where am I? . . . aye right . . . So I've decided to make this the kind of book that I would actually wanna read meself. A book with short, snappy chapters packed full of funny and outrageous stories from me life.

I mean, you don't wanna waste your time reading about me collecting stamps or getting me homework in on time! (Not that I ever did, like!) You wanna know about all the shit I got meself into as a lad, the girls I've shagged and what really goes on behind the scenes of *Geordie Shore*. That's what you really want, innit? Well, that's what you're gunna get.

But I do also wanna show you that there is another side to the Scotty T you see on TV – a softer, more thoughtful Scott (a Prince Charming you could say) that I don't think many of you have seen yet, but which maybe you saw a hint of in the

Big Brother house. So prepare to meet a version of me that you might not expect.

Anyway, enough of me banging on, let's kick clean off and take you back to when I first burst into this world. And, as you'll see, it wasn't a bundle of laughs for me mam . . .

1

I'm a Miracle!

Picture the scene ... A private room in a hospital in Gosforth (or Gossy if you're from the Toon), Newcastle, where a glamorous young woman with long, bouncy blonde hair is in the throes of labour. She groans in agony in the bed as her contractions become more and more regular, while she's watched by a doctor and a nurse who have been keeping a close eye on her since she was admitted.

'There's something not quite right here,' one of them says as they lean in a little closer and survey the situation unfolding before them. 'We may have to take some drastic action.'

Right, hang on a minute. Let's PAUSE!

Welcome to the moment the future stand-out star of *Geordie Shore* and *Celebrity Big Brother* winner, Scotty T, enters the world. We're kicking off with a bit of drama here. But, what did you expect? That I'd just pop out of me mam like a fucking lubed-up turkey, with nee botha at all? Course not!

As she'll tell you, nothing I do is ever easy, so when it came to making me debut on the scene back in 1988 I sure as hell made sure that it was a big deal. And fuck me, I really put the fear of God in her.

But first, let me give you some background info. You see, I wasn't what you'd call an everyday child. I was a miracle child. Just like Jesus, I was a gift from God.

You see, I appeared out of the blue, without warning. I was never meant to exist, man. But as a result of being such a massive surprise to me mam Gill and me dad Rob, I also managed to cause 'em a few extra worries along the way. And I would continue to do so over the next 28 years!

How? Well, that's complicated. You see a couple of years before, me mam had suffered an ectopic pregnancy and had been told that it was very unlikely she'd be able to have another kid. She was gutted of course, but she and Dad kept banging without a thought about having another kid. Then in September of 1987, me mam found out she was knocked up! With fucking me! What a result, eh Scotty T?

Of course, for the next nine months Mam was shitting herself with fear in case anything went wrong. But it all seemed to go all right until the day her waters broke.

Just like Jesus, I was a gift from God.

Dad rushed Mam into Princess Mary Maternity Hospital to have me. But when the doctors had a look up me mam's chuff they could see that there was something not quite right.

10

I was upside down. According to the doctors I was breech, which meant I was feet down in me mam's stomach (i.e., not the ideal way of passing through a woman's business end), and was sitting in her tummy with me knees bent up into me chest! To start with, they tried to ease me out the normal way but apparently it could have been dangerous for me. Instead, they suggested that they knock me mam out and give her a Caesarean, which she said she was more than happy to do.

Question: Do you think cos I wasn't born through a fanny, that explains why I have spent most me life trying to get back into as many as I can? . . . RITES!

Mam was thrilled when she found out I was a boy. Her and me dad had an agreement – if it had been a girl she would have picked the name. A boy and it was Dad's choice. And he picked Scott. Cheers Dad!

It wasn't long before I was home, sucking on me mam's chebs and being a rather obedient little baby! I might have been that well-behaved little fella in these early days, but me mam and dad were soon to discover that they were in for a nightmare once I started to grow up . . .

2

MAM HOOVERS UP HARRY!

So the year was 1988. Teen pin-ups Kylie and Jason had the nation weeping buckets when they tied the knot on *Neighbours*, popstar Yazz had kids bopping away in discos to her chart-topper (and future *TOWIE* theme tune) 'The Only Way Is Up' and some old rascal called Maggie Thatcher was continuing to piss everyone off up and down the country with her dodgy policies.

Of course, I was too busy shitting and pissing meself to be aware of any of that, but I'm just trying to set the scene for you! All I was interested in back then was getting me mouth around me mam's tit when I was hungry! Now, as I told you earlier, way before I could even walk or talk, I had caused me mam and dad nee end of trouble. A sure sign of things to come! But when me parents brought me home they were only too happy to have a healthy baby finally in their lives after all they had gone through with the ectopic pregnancy.

Me first house was on Jubilee Road in the semi-snooty area

of Gosforth – a neighbourhood to the north of Newcastle city centre. Me parents had only recently moved out of a flat just under a mile away to accommodate the new super-sized pram they had bought in preparation for me arrival.

I have vague recollections of red carpets, mad rugs, cream sofas and a garden, but I was so young, I could be wrong. Me mam, however, recalls that the house was nowt special, describing it as neither too big, nor too small but just right for a new young family – and from the sounds of it, fucking Goldilocks.

In the early days, I was apparently as good as gold; a baby who would sleep when I was supposed to and eat when I needed to. So absolutely nee trouble.

But it wasn't long before I started having a pure frisk cos by the time I was nine months old, I'd swiftly progressed from crawling along the floor on all fours to bopping around on two feet. RESULT! Which meant I could get around quite freely and without anyone's assistance.

While that was great for me and me newfound sense of freedom, it was not so great for me parents, who found it hard to keep track of me. Or at least me mam, who was stuck with me on her own most of the time.

You see, me dad worked away for about two or three weeks every month on the oil rigs in the North Sea. He was a commercial diver whose job was, among other things, to weld pipes at the bottom of the sea. Very technical and dangerous stuff! Mam, meanwhile, had been working at the *Evening Chronicle* in the sales and advertising department until quitting a few weeks before I was born. She would later go back when I was two and I had started nursery.

Anyway, where was I? By nine months old, it was like I was a part of fucking *Spellbound*, doing all sorts of acrobatics round the house like I'd been up walking for years, pure natural. But with this newfound mobility, also came a taste for adventure and mischief, which would stick with me for the rest of me life.

Cos I can't remember shit all that well, here's me mam to tell you more . . .

MAM: So he had started to walk at nine months, and he was running around all the time. It was impossible to keep up with him. And he was a right inquisitive little fella. You'd sit him down for a second, and the minute your back was turned, he'd be up and running around and trying to get into cupboards for sweets. Worried that he'd end up drinking a bottle of bleach or something, I had to put locks on all the cupboards to keep him out. But what do you know – the little devil was able to unlock them. Ooh, he was a clever little boy.

But as he got a bit older, more of the real Scott started to shine through and he was a cheeky little bugger! I remember this one time he must have been coming up to one year old and I had him sat in his high chair. While I was preparing his food, he was looking at me smiling that gorgeous smile of his and flashing those beautiful big bright eyes. I sat down to feed him and gave him his plastic baby fork to feed himself – he was very advanced, don't forget – but instead of gobbling up his baby mush, he fired it at me like a catapult, and spattered it all over me nice clean top. That'll teach me! The boy was trouble.

I knew this was just the start of things to come. And I was right.

When I took him out, he was even more of a handful. While I'd be looking through aisles in a shop he'd wriggle his way out of the pushchair, dart straight over to the pick 'n' mix shelves and start grabbing handfuls of sweets for himself. I was so embarrassed that I sometimes had to pretend he wasn't mine!

> '*I was so embarrassed that I sometimes had to pretend he wasn't mine!' – Gill*

I can remember pushing him around Marks & Spencer – he'd be dragging clothes off the racks and shoving them in the pushchair! Luckily I'd notice what he was up to before the store security had me hauled up for shoplifting. He was a wicked little boy, but you couldn't help but fall in love with him.

When I was around two years old, me mam took me to a private nursery school in Gosforth for three days a week while she went back to the *Chronicle* part-time. It was here, me mam tells me, where I really came into me own.

I'd love doing jigsaws, the harder the better. In fact, me skills at piecing together these puzzles impressed me teachers so much that one day they actually took me mam aside to tell her how amazed they were that I had mastered puzzles designed for children aged fucking seven and above – go on, son! As a result, they told her, they had had to restock the nursery with puzzles for older kids just for me!

Apparently, whenever I had something to do to occupy me mind at nursery, I was at me happiest. I liked doing things and being kept busy, and when I was, I was nee trouble to anyone. But sit me on a mat with the other kids and read me a story and I couldn't be fucked! I'd be up and about looking for something else to do or trying to climb out the window or putting me hand up and asking stupid questions that I didn't really want the answers to. I could, the nursery staff told me mam, be quite a handful.

Back home, I liked playing with me Scalextric set. I was good at building things by now, so I was pretty nifty at piecing together the massive and intricate racetrack. And when the cars were in place, there was nee Sunday nanna driving from me. I went from nought to 60 in about a second and watched as me race car shot around the track like a pure rocket. Most of the time, I'd crank up the speed so much that the cars would just shoot off the tracks every time they took a turn, then after that I'd start launching them about. Now that was fun for me!

Around this time, when I was three or four, I had a pet hamster called Harry who joined the family. I dunno what else to say about him, except that he was a hamster. A little furry fucker with tiny legs. But I pure loved Harry, me, and I used to love looking at him do fuck all in his cage, just sitting there. So, sometimes, as a treat, I'd take him out and stuff him into this hamster ball thing and watch him go mad spinning around the room like a little trooper. I even gave him some extra entertainment with the odd volley down the stairs. He loved a bit of hamster zorbing, Harry did!

I remember one day, I was in me room doing summat or other while me mam was busy hoovering the house. I went to go and see her and when I walked into the living room I could see Mam was really giving the carpet a good seeing to, so much so that there was gunna be nowt left of the thing. She nodded but cos she looked busy I turned to go back to me room. But as I did, I noticed that Harry's cage was empty and the door was wide open – the little bastard had got out. I looked at Mam who was still hoovering without a care in the world. All of a sudden I put two and two together. Open cage + nee hamster + Mam going aka with the Hoover = Deed Harry!

'Mam!' I was full-on screaming, trying to get her attention over the sound of that daft vacuum. 'Where's Harry, Mam?'

Mam just smiled at me and made a gesture with the Hoover. Now to a kid of me age, who was already anxious about the wellbeing of his wicked pet, I came to think her gesture was suggesting that she'd sucked Harry up in the Hoover on purpose. I was going absolutely mental, 'What you doing, Mam?!'

As it hit me that me furry pal might be dead, me face propa creased up, tears began to flow and I started to boot off. And with a set of lungs like mine, you can imagine the noise. Nearly put the windows out. That Hoover was nee competition.

Mam noticed I was foaming, turned off the Hoover and asked me what was wrong. 'Here, man, you've sucked up

Harry,' I wept. 'I have not,' she replied. 'Look, Scott, he's over there.' She pointed across the room and there he was, the little maddo having the time of his life in that little ball of his. That was a nightmare over. Anyways, I was so buzzing that he wasn't gone I went to comfort him. Harry?! . . . KICK!!!

3

ACTION MAN SCOTTY

I love me mam and dad, I really do. But like many young boys, I think I felt closest to me mam growing up, even though me dad is an absolute ledge. Even to this day she's still the most important woman in me life. And probably always will be.

Of course, I was the apple of her eye and we spent so much time together that, according to Mam, I would let only her read to me cos I don't think me dad had the patience to tell the story properly. If he tried to, then I'd be adamant that I wasn't having it and would say to him, 'Nah, I want Mam to read it.' (I don't actually think this is entirely true or if it's just Mam's cheeky way at getting back at Dad since – SPOILER ALERT – they got divorced. But that's what she says anyways!)

I'm still not sure if the bond between me and me mam was stronger cos Dad was away on the rigs a lot, but me and her were pretty tight. Don't get me wrong, I loved me dad so much – he was amazing and we have had and still do have unreal times together – but me and Mam had a stronger bond at the time, with him being away. Me dad – fair play to him – would be grafting his arse off for weeks on end and when he came home he would still be adamant about spending every day with me doing loads of fun shit and buying me anything I wanted, propa spoilt I was. This was the way it was and I wasn't exactly complaining.

When I was norty, I knew which of the two of them I could wrap round me little finger best. If Mam told me off, I'd just start putting on the water works and within two minutes she'd soften up and let me off, whereas me dad was the stricter of the two with the shorter temper just like me, as you will find out later. If I was bad, he would propa bollock us, but if I was good – and I was occasionally – he would always sing me praises and spend loads of coins on us.

But nee matter how range me dad went with me, I would always find it in me heart to forgive him straight away when he came home from the rigs with loads of great gifts for me, like Scalextric and Lego and ki-ki-ki-K'Nexaaaa kits (bit of mc'ing there, sorry!).

I fucking loved Lego you nah, cos I loved building shit. I would literally sit there for hours just constructing all sorts of madness. It kept me mind busy and focused and most of the time out of trouble, and I'd stick with it until I'd finished what I was making. I would build the best stuff, like pure pirate ships, castles and full-on cities … you name it. Whatever Lego kit was put in front of me I would start going mad assembling it in record time and not look up until it was done. When I had completed each Lego challenge, I saw it as a laugh just to smash it up and start all over again, or start building me own creations, which I was propa mint at. I really think I was at me happiest and chilled when I was doing this. And I'd spend literally hours playing with Lego or K'NEX, long into the evening, cos the last thing I wanted to do was to go to bed. Going to sleep was boring. A lot of the time I'd just pretend to go to sleep, wait till me mam and dad were in bed, get up and start partying with me Lego again. It was going off! There was so much life to live, man.

When I wasn't creating something lethal, I liked to spend some of me time playing with me Action Man, which reminded me a lot of meself. Cos I loved the *Rambo* and *Predator* films so much, which I'd already seen on video, I would pretend me little plastic soldier was taking on some invisible evil bloke who was threatening to destroy the world, and other times I would take over from Action Man being the protector and I'd jump in and start scrapping with pillows and that, running around the house like I was chasing fucking Casper. What a little hero I was!

I would point me fingers and fire imaginary bullets out of them or wave around any object I could substitute – a gun like a piece of wood or a fucking spatula – but there were a few times when I managed to actually get me hands on a real gun! Can you believe it? Nee, neither could I! The guns belonged to Dad, back when you could have a propa licence to keep one. I think he also used them when he had worked away in Nigeria offshore on the rigs for protection. He had these stashed around the house away from view but there was a few times he would surprise me and show me them, letting me only play with the ones he had disabled so that when I did come across them, they wouldn't cause any harm.

When I saw one, I couldn't believe it. I mean, it's not every day you see propa guns in real life, just in films on the telly. I remember holding it in me hand and thinking how big it looked between me little fingers. It was heavier than I thought it would be and even though I was quite young, I knew just how deadly it could be if it was in full working order, and there's me waving them around just like the action heroes I'd seen on the telly did, shouting fucking 'Pow! Pow!' but I knew there was nothing to be worried about.

Dad was a real man's man, tough and masculine, and a little impatient. Bloody hell, he used to have a pet crocodile at one point, from what I saw from a couple of photos I once found lying around! Pure photos of him taking it on walks and that's nee joke: one of his pals had an actual arctic wolf. Swell, mental! But me dad was a really good dad and I think I am definitely a chip off the old block.

He was a really good dad and I think I am definitely a chip off the old block.

Like me, he had an eye for the ladies and I think back in the day when he was younger he was a bit of a player. Or so me mam suggested, telling me that when they first met, he had been – how can I say? – a little over-familiar with her. Go on, Dad!

MAM: I was 24 and living with me mam and dad in Darras Hall. After a night out on the town with some pals, me and a girlfriend came back to mine cos me parents were away and she insisted on bringing her boyfriend with her, a guy called Rob. This Rob was a handsome fella, with a nice head of thick dark hair. But even though he was properly seeing me friend, it didn't stop the cheeky bastard from making a grab for me bum while she was out of the way and trying to get me in the broom cupboard.

See, the apple doesn't fall far from the tree! Like father like son, aye.

As Mam's not like me, she was having none of it; she brushed him off and that was that! Cockblocked to the max! But that wasn't the last she saw of him. A year later, the pair of them bumped into each other again on a night out in town. But this time, he was single. Still interested in me mam, he asked her out, she agreed and the pair went off to a local Italian for a romantic meal. But, as is the way of our family, drama was never too far behind. When they arrived at the restaurant, me mam started down the steps to the entrance, but instead of a graceful descent, she tripped and went arse over tit and ended up black and blue all over her legs and arms – nightmare for the kid! Yet, in spite of their disastrous first date, the two of them hit it off, married a year or so later and the rest is history.

To make up for his time working away on the rigs, me dad would plan some male bonding time for the two of us.

Sometimes, he would take me to see a film, or other times we'd travel across Newcastle to go and see his mam and dad and me cousins. But every so often he would take me away for a week or so.

On a few of these occasions, Dad splashed out and took the two of us away somewhere fancy. On one particular occasion, we flew to Canada to see his brother who was head of an army base over there. I was really excited about the trip as it was one of me first propa trips abroad. I loved everything about the journey, especially the flight. I was a typical boy; I just loved the idea of us jetting across the sky 40,000 feet above people like me mam back on the ground who were going about their business, cracking on with their cups of tea at home.

When we arrived in Calgary, it was like nowhere I had seen before. Well I had, but only in magazines and on the telly. It was fucking freezing, which reminded me very much of home. And while the city part of it looked normal, the backdrop of snowcapped mountains was pretty impressive. It looked like a pure postcard with me, innit!

Me dad's brother was a sergeant or whatever in the army. I'm not very good with the ranks, but he was a really important fella in the barracks. Like Dad, he was very masculine, just as you'd expect a military man to be. I couldn't see him at first cos he was camouflaged, man it propa confused me! The people around him would address him in a really formal way, which I found funny as to me he was just me big uncle Jimmy. But he was quality and he gave us a tour of his barracks where I even got the chance to sit in one of the tanks.

It was like a dream come true to be sitting in this beast of a machine. Up close, it was bigger than I ever expected it to be (maybe cos I was still a kid) and was a pretty scary sight when you saw it up close. I mean, imagine something like that hurtling towards you in a war – I'd fucking cake meself! But it didn't take long before I was scaling the roof and climbing up into the cockpit, fiddling with all the controls and moving the turret like I was doing fucking dot-to-dot on the wall on the other side of the room. I felt like king of the world. Inside, though, I was surprised to see just how much of a tight squeeze it was, like. I couldn't imagine how the hell they end up getting two or three fully grown soldiers squashed in there when they were off to war, they'd almost be sucking each other off it was that cramped – I couldn't get me head around it. But then again, it was for battle, not for having a few bevvies, a kip or a shag.

After hanging out with me uncle and his family for a couple of days, Dad and I headed off to a place called Banff, a small town in the Rocky Mountains west of Calgary, to go skiing. I remember that we drove along frosty roads surrounded by thick snow and then came to a part of the road where we suddenly saw this amazing-looking lake that had a waterfall cascading into it. It was such an unforgettable sight to see, seriously it's stuck in me head – certainly nowt like I'd see back home in Gossy. The biggest waterfall you'd see back home would be in some rich bloke's fucking bird bath in their back garden. By the edges of this pond I remember seeing beavers building dams. I dunno why I remember this particular scene so much, like, but it's one memory of childhood that really sticks in me head in full HD-quality vividness. Perhaps it was just a sign of things to come – as obviously beavers would one day become such an integral part of me life!

In Banff, Dad and I hung out at the Hard Rock Café, took a dip at the local swimming pool and had unreal meals in a restaurant high up in the mountains that boasted absolutely spectacular views of the mountains. I really did feel like I was in a different world from home. And it made me begin to realise that there was a bigger world outside of the one I knew. That Newcastle, the place I loved and called home, wasn't the be all and end all. There was more out there to explore.

Later, we hit the ski slopes. That's right, never mind learning to walk at an early age I was fucking skiing early as well. I'd never been skiing on propa snow before, just dry slopes back in Newcastle. I was buzzing me tits off and nervous at the same time at what was about to follow. I was by no means an expert even though I thought I was, I was able to stay upright on two skis, which in me mind was all that mattered. So when we got to the slopes, Dad got us fitted out in ski clobber and skis and said, 'Stick closely to me and don't go wandering off on your own.'

The second me skis touched the snow, I felt like the real deal and as expected, I took to the snow like Al Pacino. I think I'm one of those lads who has sportiness streaming through their veins. I've always taken to any sport with ease. Yee name it, I can do it. Especially bollock naked leap frogging – one of me favourites! In later years at school, I would win medals for swimming and I became a sports day legend at middle school – but more on that later, like. I keep getting carried away.

After I was skiing for a while, I think I started to become a bit cocky. The more I got used to the skis and snow, the more confident I became. Too confident, in fact. During one run on the slopes, for a laugh I thought I'd speed up, leaving me dad behind. TEE-RAH DAD! I was pure hurling down this slope, realised that I was definitely losing control cos I wasn't able to slow meself down. In fact, as I shot down the piste, I realised I was actually gaining more speed! I started to panic for bit but then just accepted it as there was nowt I could do.

I was desperately trying to angle me skis the way I had been taught, to help slow me down (the plough or whatever it's called), but cos of the crazy speed I was going at it wasn't happening for me, like. As I was blaring down I saw a jump looming before me. Me heart started racing even more than it was before. What should I do? Should I risk the jump or should I try to topple over to stop meself before I reached the edge? Nah, I'm not being a bitch toppling over, I'm gunna go for it. So here we go, reaching the edge, I suddenly felt me skis leave the snow beneath me feet. For a moment, there was this weird silence, followed by a full-on thud. It wasn't the ground, no, it was a fucking fence! Unable to bring meself to a stop I managed to smash the bottom half of me body into the fence and do a full-on scorpion into the ground. I didn't even slide further, there was just me with me heed stuck in the ground like a fucking deformed ostrich. What a belta!

Regaining me composure, I properly seen the fence that I'd crashed into and I also noticed the massive signs saying 'no skiing' and 'route not permitted' about five metres in front of the hill – the route I was actually skiing towards, what a divvy I was. Strangely, I couldn't help but think to meself that it had been one of the most exhilarating things I had ever experienced, even though I could have propa hurt meself. But I didn't, and the thrill of the danger had really given me an adrenaline rush. I knew that I wanted that feeling from now on again and again, and when I attended me first school, me unsuspecting teachers were about to find out just how much of a handful this kid could be.

4

FIRST SCHOOL TERROR

Anyone who says they enjoyed their first day of primary school is either lying or a propa gimp! School is pure shit, right, and when it's your first day of primary, it's like the worst torture in the world cos you are being ripped away from constant fun and the comforts of your own home. So when Mam and Dad took to me to Linden First School in Forest Hall (people in Newcastle will know it's been knocked down now ... thank fuck, dunno what they're gunna be building in its place, probably get turned into a car park like everywhere else, or most likely open up another Greggs on top of the seven hundred that are already in Newcastle). Anyways, arriving at primary school I made sure everyone in the school knew I wasn't happy about it. Already late for the registration, me parents literally had to drag me along the corridors to me first class, as I refused to walk anywhere. Me parents weren't best pleased at all, like. I was going mad, kicking and screaming me little heed off cos there was nee chance I wanted to go at all. I think they were pretty embarrassed and I could tell that once they got me in the classroom they were just gunna dump me into the teacher's hands and take straight off.

As I got in the class, all the other kids were just pure sat in their seats giving me hacky looks with red eyes of their own, looking at me like I was some sort of absolute crack-pot cos I was wriggling and screaming like I was being kidnapped. The teacher came over, took me hand and attempted to lead me over to the other kids. But I wasn't having it. Instead, I screamed, 'Naaaaa!' at the top of me voice. Eventually me mam took me to one side, told me how much fun I was going to have with all the other kids and that I could look forward to her cooking me favourite tea when I got home that afternoon. I wasn't buying what she was saying, like, I didn't even have a favourite tea cos I liked everything. But, I could see the wailing and screaming wasn't doing me any favours, so I pulled meself together and stubbornly sat in a chair at the back of the class where I remained relatively quiet for the rest of the day. The kids must of thought ... what an arsehole! BOTHERED!

Linden was a private school, which Mam paid for out of her own money. I was her only child so she wanted me to have the best education I could have. She had heard the school had a great reputation and small classes, so she reckoned I would be given more attention there than I would at a bigger school. Unfortunately it was also a school with a pretty minging uniform. I had to wear dark green sweater with a yellow stripe, grey shorts with a matching cap. I fucking hated that cap, like – always tried to make dogs eat the thing. No sooner had Mam stuck it on me head, then I'd launch it like a Frisbee. It was shit.

The school building was pretty impressive to look at, but then again I was four and anything looked impressive to me at this time, even a rock. It was a big white building with pipes coming out of it from all angles, with about six chimneys on different parts of the place. Inside, it was propa old-fashioned, with lots of wooden trimmings and furnishings and a ridiculously old staircase that looked like it belonged in a Harry Potter film.

Me classroom was in the attic, where there was a dusty old blackboard, twenty small chairs and those propa old-fashioned wooden school desks that lift open, with random people's writing all over them: 'Dale loves fucking Harriet 4 eva and eva', 'Scotty T was fucking ere '95' – all that shit! Downstairs in the yard there was lots of metal fencing. To be honest, it looked more like a building site than a playground, but there was a gap in the fence which you could sneak through into a field where the grass was long and rarely cut. It was like following fucking Bear Grylls through the Amazon trying to walk through it. I remember when it finally did get cut we all started chucking grass at each other and making kids eat it. Of course we all got in trouble.

It was around this time that I started to notice girls as well, ohhh aye! Obviously me interaction with girls back then was a bit more innocent than it is now – no one was playing me like a trumpet at Linden. But there was a girl there who had caught me eye. Sadly, I can't really tell you what she looked

31

like or even remember her name – I think it was Julie – but if you were this lucky girl and you remember me please get in touch. Nothing like a bit of unfinished business if you nah what I mean.

I remember following this girl around the school and I had convinced meself that I was totally and madly in love with her, whatever that means when you're bloody four years old! And it seemed that she liked me too cos she quite happily joined me behind one of the mobile classrooms and kissed me on the lips. Obviously with nee tongues. I think! Unfortunately I can't say how I felt about the kiss, I can't remember if I got a stiffy or not, but I must have liked it cos we carried on doing it again and again and again! MINT!

As I got a bit older, me behaviour at school became what you might call erratic. During classes I was very distracted and always getting up to something I shouldn't. If we were reading in class, I just couldn't be arsed and I would look out of the window, carve me name into me wooden desk or hoy stuff at people in the room – anything that meant I didn't have to read a fucking book! Books bored me. I mean, what's the point of books when you can watch the telly? Wey, except this one of course! OBVS!

While reading might not have really 'floated me boat', maths was a whole different kettle of fish. Maths came easy to me and I think I liked it as much as building shit out of Lego and causing trouble. I dunno why I did cos I know most people hate maths with a passion. But for me, I just got it. I loved doing long division and when I was given stuff like that to work out I would just rock it. I loved doing times tables too. For me, getting me head around numbers was easy cos me mind was suddenly engaged and I really enjoyed it. But I think this interest had something to do with me granddad (on me mam's side), who I will introduce you to later.

But school was not the best of places. Let me put it out there now. It was boring. And I really didn't care what was going on. And after a while teachers picked up on me slack attitude and they would tell me off and send me to the headmaster.

Now this was an establishment which turned out to be a bit radge – there was a teacher who would stalk the building carrying a strap or a cane and wander into class unexpectedly just to see if we were behaving well, I swear to God. To be honest, I can't remember exactly why I got the strap, but I think it was probably for not listening or cos I was shouting in class or something, which I did a fair amount of.

I remember one time when the teacher paced up and down in front of his desk tapping the strap into his hand. I think he was trying to intimidate me, which he did a little bit, but I sure as hell wasn't going to let him know that. So I put on a brave face and took it like a man. God, it fucking hurt, like, I wanted to strangle him with it at the time, but I held me own. There were times, however, when I couldn't hide me feelings and I'd bawl like a baby!

But it wasn't all bad. If we were good in class, we were rewarded with sweets. They were called Mojos and when I was good and rewarded with these sweets I was loving life. Talk about bribery! Do you remember those Mojo sweets?

Well, we'd get them. And if I didn't get one for being good, well, I just used to nick them instead from this tuck shop, which was literally a hole in a wall like a sideways toilet. Ah, I remember it well. Like a pure soldier, I'd sneak in through this hole in the wall and grab handfuls of sweets like Chomps, Freddos, Curly Wurlys, the fucking lot. I rarely got caught, but when I did, well, you know what happened – THWAP! – a cane across the back of me legs, not even joking.

Eventually me behaviour became so erratic that me mam was called into the school for a chat. As it turned out it was THE chat! They wanted to expel me. Why? I honestly can't remember. I really can't as everything I did kind of blurred into one.

MAM: So they said to me that Scott was removed from the school cos they just couldn't handle him. They said he was running around everywhere and there just wasn't the room for him to be him. They said that he didn't listen in class, that he did his own thing and he was always putting his hand up in class and interrupting and asking questions. So then they'd send him out of the classroom for doing that.

It was THE chat! They wanted to expel me.

When I heard this I thought, well that's just an inquisitive child. Surely that's the kind of thing they'd wanna encourage in school! But it would seem not! His dad was furious, and stormed up to the school and told them exactly

34

what he thought about the situation; that they were out of order for not being able to look after Scott and they were not understanding or encouraging in any way.

In the end, we decided to remove him. The one thing I will say about that school is that it was good for his education but not good for him as a person. So we moved him to Gosforth First School.

Now this new school was a lot better for me. It was a lot less strict, it was bigger and more modern. The building was all one level, with glass roofs and everything. The kids were more of a laugh and down to earth, and I was given this red material briefcase thing to carry around and put me work in – I felt important. One vivid memory I have is of this one poor girl just standing in the middle of the playground and pissing herself in front of the whole school! I was like, eh what's going on? What a frisk! Funny to think that years later, I'd end up sharing a house on a TV show with 25-year-old lasses who'd piss the bed every night. Girls who wet themselves seem to be a part of me life, as it goes. ILL!

Gosforth was where I came into me own and started to make some propa pals. Two lads I hit it off with immediately were called Alex Bell and Adam Stark. Alex was tall and skinny with a blond streak, Adam was a shorter and skinnier lad with brown hair. They weren't exactly what you'd call the super cool crew. Geeky is probably a better word, but who knows at that time. You didn't exactly know what's what back then but they were good lads.

There was another kid in the school who caught me eye.

He was a black guy called Sam Epsenay and from what I could see he seemed to be a good crack. Now, let me just put this out there straight away. Due to me limited experience of the world, I had never actually seen a black guy in the flesh before or noticed anyone of a different race, and I was that young that I didn't understand that the world was even made up of different races. Don't forget this was the north east back in the '90s. Anyway, me and this kid started to hang out with each other on school break times. He seemed like a cool guy and I really wanted to be his mate. But one day, when we were running across the yard just doing what little boys do I started shouting after him, 'Blackie! Blackie!'

Of course, I thought nothing of it until a while after a teacher took me to one side and told me Sam had told her that the words I was using had upset him and warned me that if I continued to use them I'd be in big trouble. Now, I was used to getting told off for misbehaving but never for making someone feel bad about themselves and I was mortified and said, 'Oh, I'm sorry, I didn't realise what I was saying.' And then I think I started crying cos I was a bit shocked. But honestly, I didn't know any different back then.

Anyway, in the end, after that drama, me and Sam started talking to each other and we became dead pally. He'd come round to mine and I would go round to his and play basketball in his yard with his little brother Stephen.

Both our sets of parents became good friends. Sam's mam Jackie would bake bread for us and bring it in to school, while his dad Anthony was an ophthalmologist, who could look into someone's eyes and see what was wrong with them.

Very clever. Mam said he was spot on when he looked into her eyes and was even able to tell her about a second ectopic pregnancy she endured.

Sam and I would hang out with Alex and Adam and play in the woods behind his house, making rope swings so that we could cross the river. We were right little adventurers in our spare time, just like mini Ray Mears. Even at school we were at home with nature and used to gather round the small pond in the school yard and hunt for tadpoles. Of course, as we were little rascals, we also had a habit of pushing each other into the little pond which was canny fucking deep, and then when we climbed out we'd be covered in leeches. The teachers, naturally enough, were not amused.

Us lads loved watching films. We would go to the cinema or have sleepover nights at Alex's and Adam's house where we'd watch films and daft cartoons like *Dexter's Laboratory* and *Ed, Edd n Eddy* – a cartoon about three friends, one of whom speaks to a fucking plank of wood – that would send the three of us psychotic. It's mad how entertaining it actually was. The other cartoon was about some little nerd called Dexter who got bullied by his sister DeeDee but he had a secret lab in his house and used to always be down with loads of mad science shit. Sometimes, we'd even freak ourselves out and watch horror films like *Halloween*, *The Shining* or *Child's Play* (the one with the radge little ginger doll that used to go round topping people)!

5

THE MAN WHO CHANGED ME LIFE

Did it come as a surprise to you that I really love maths, then? I bet you never expected me to say that. I mean, maths is the least sexy subject at school, like. But for me . . . well, it's what makes me mind actually kick into gear and focus as I was actually a genius at it. Books and that can do off and gan read themselves. Give me a fuck-off long equation or long division anytime and I'll box it clean off.

As I've already said, I have me granddad to thank for me interest in figures and sums. He was an engineer back in the day which is where he got his mass intelligence from. He'd be the one who showed me everything I needed to know and how far me brain could be stretched.

Richard Baxter was me mam's dad and a total legend. Of all the people in me life I reckon he's the one who has understood me the most. He knew I could be a crafty little shit who got into trouble at school or up to mischief at home. But for some reason, when I was with him and me nan Sheila I was like a totally different person. He managed to do the impossible – he calmed me down and stopped me head from spinning. He had so much patience with me.

As I got older, I was becoming more and more boisterous, more fidgety and even more distracted. But when I went to see Granddad, all of a sudden I became a lot more well behaved. I dunno why but he had this amazing hold over me. He never treated me like a kid, never raised his voice to me and only ever encouraged me to be the best I could. He had the most patience with me, without a doubt. He could see that as I was slowly growing up something was going on in me head that no one could quite put their finger on, but instead of just dismissing it as me being a pre-teen horror, he always tried to calm me down and understand me.

When I used to get into trouble at school or at home, Mam and Dad would tend to lose it with me, but not Granddad. He knew what I was like, what I was *really* like, and he would take me to one side, sit me down and play games with me. Sometimes he'd show me how to do card tricks – daft ones, but they'd keep me entertained for hours. He and me nan loved bridge so he taught me to play that too, as well as poker and gin rummy. In fact, I was fast becoming a bit of a games demon. When we weren't trying to outwit each other, Granddad would give me maths problems to get me head round which kept me pretty occupied. If anyone else had tried to get me to do some long sums at home, in me free time, I'd have laughed and told them to fuck reet off. But for Granddad, I'd do anything.

Granddad would also help me with me homework. If I told him I couldn't do something, he'd say to me, 'Yes you can.' He wouldn't take no for an answer. He would never give me the solutions; he'd encourage me to work them out for meself and tell me that I just had to think about it. For him, I would always be fully dedicated. However, sometimes, I'd be stumped by something and cos I felt like I was being pushed into a corner mentally and could not see a way out, I would run off and watch the telly. But then the feeling that I was letting me granddad down crept into me head and I'd skulk back to him, sit meself down again and get back to it until these problems were solved.

For Granddad, I'd do anything.

But it wasn't all hard work at me nan and granddad's. I used to go round to their place every Friday night without fail and got treated like royalty, but never spoilt. Nan would make me anything I wanted to eat, even takeaways, or buy me whatever sweets I wanted from the shops. Every morning without fail it would be sausage and bacon sandwiches, or mebbies even a Spam one ... KEEMON. She knew what I liked and she made sure I got it.

As I chomped away on any amounts of scran, I would sit with them and watch that week's *Top of the Pops* (yeah, it was still popular back then). Sometimes we'd watch that *Fawlty Towers* and, although it might have been a 20-year-old sitcom by then, it still made me crease. Then, after me supper, I'd nip upstairs to watch something like *Men Behaving Badly* on me nan's telly (taking tips no doubt for the future – not that I needed any). I loved it! I still bop away to the theme tune! If me nan wasn't shooing me off to bed early, I'd get comfy, settle down and watch *Eurotrash*!

Presented by two French guys, Antoine de Caunes and fashion designer Jean Paul Gaultier, viewers would be introduced to a bunch of weirdos from across Europe showing off some oddball pastime or skill, most usually naked. And that's why us lads loved the show so much. It was our only chance to check out lush European lasses with huge tits bouncing on trampolines and that. Not just big tits, mind, but massive, humungous ones that looked like melons, a lot of them had hairy fannies as well. At this time I didn't nah the difference, but as I learnt later in life I couldn't go wrong with a smooth landing strip.

I remember one woman on the show was called Lolo Ferrari. She was a blonde dancer, porno actress and singer who had fuck-loads of surgery to increase her bust to a Guinness World Record size. She looked like a freak, but when you're a kid who's barely seen a bird's body, you think she is like the most perfect woman you've ever seen and you wished that she was jumping up and down right in front of you or sitting on you. It was a really stupid programme but, like any boy me age, I used to get propa horny over it and I fucking loved every filthy minute of it. Come on Channel 4, bring it back again!!

The morning after I stayed over, me and Granddad would walk to the same paper shop he went to every day. He'd buy his newspapers, then once he was outside he'd say to me,

'Breathe in, breathe out, take ten deep breaths and hold each one in for ten seconds.' He loved being out in the open air. He was an active man and he loved going on long walks. For a man in his early seventies, he was very fit and healthy. I thought me granddad was invincible.

Sometimes we used to walk up this dirt road from the Diamond Inn in Ponteland that led to a farm at the back of the golf course, miles and miles. We'd walk past the farm and I would jump around in the hay bales for a bit, then we'd climb over a fence and walk along this really long dirt path some more, then we'd climb over another gate and some-times walk all the way to Dinnington, then turn around and head back home. By the time we made it back, I'd be exhausted and Granddad, well, he looked unfazed. He loved the idea of breathing in fresh air every once in a while, even though he smoked a pipe – a pipe that I would take a few drags on when he wasn't watching!

In spite of his age, Granddad was a pretty dapper bloke. Yes, he had a headful of white hair and always wore granda caps, but he looked propa smart all the time. Wherever he went he would slip on a smart jacket and shove a handkerchief in the pocket. He always looked ready to meet the Queen!

I think he was proud of his life journey. Mam told me that Granddad had a hard life growing up. His family had pretty much nothing and lived in a shabby terrace house in Byker, which isn't the nicest area of Newcastle. It was the kind of house that had a machine out in the back where you turn a handle to wring your wet washing out. He was 19 when his dad died and he decided to make something of himself. He worked very hard, taking courses, putting himself through night school, doing degrees. He even had elocution lessons.

And it worked cos he ended up getting a job at big industrial company, Parsons, in the engineering bit before becoming an area manager for big oil company Shell. He really was what you'd call a self-made man. But he actually almost had a career as a footballer. When he was younger he played for the Newcastle United boys team, but nothing came of it. Instead, he played golf regularly – his biggest passion aside from his wife Sheila and the family – and won several cups along the way. Granddad even taught me to play golf! Again, I bet you didn't think I'd enjoy taking part in a sport like that! But for Granddad, I would do anything. He'd take me to the golf club near where he lived in Ponteland and showed me how to get a good swing. He was so encouraging and he always told me that he was happy when I did well.

While he might not have made it as a professional sportsman, Granddad found pure joy in me nan, who made him the happiest man in the world. He didn't need trophies or money to make him happy. All he ever wanted was the love of a good woman and that's what he got. They met when they were both working at Parsons, where she was a draughtswoman, and fell in love and got married. Then they had me mam and me uncle, then moved the family to Harrogate for a few years before coming back to a nice part of Ponteland and living happily ever after.

Aww ... So lesson learned, boys and girls. Love is what makes the world go round. But so does a fucking dirty cocktail!

6

THERE'S SOMETHING WRONG WITH SCOTT!

Enjoying the book so far? Just making sure, like. I wouldn't want you to think it was one of those dead boring ones, like.

I'm glad you've finally got to meet me family; they really are the most important people in me world. But don't worry party crew, there's loads more action to come and some right fit lads – i.e. me mates – for you to meet, not to mention some radge action that will make your hair stand on end and some shocks that will make you think 'WHAT THE FUCK?!?!'

But anyway, let's crack on.

By the time I was seven me mam and dad had moved us to a lovely little bungalow in Blackheath Court, on Tudor Grange in Kingston Park. It was a lovely place that had a big garden. At the end of it was a line of conifer trees that stood like soldiers all along the back fence and behind them was a massive field with really long grass I called 'the mown', which was the perfect place to take me new dog Holly for a run.

Holly was a wicked little Border Collie who was so full of energy. I loved taking her out into the fields and watching her run wild. Of course, I used get a buzz from winding her up so much I would tease the thing to the max. Once I whipped out a tennis ball she would freeze, then I'd launch it as far as I could and watch Holly nash after it, and I would hide while she was chasing it but she would always manage to find me.

Dutifully she'd always bring the ball back in her teeth and drop it, covered in dog spaff. I would throw it again, this time further away than the last (or so she'd think cos I'd just pretend to throw and piss meself laughing as I watched her dart to the left and to the right thinking I'd actually let go of the ball). Sometimes when she would bring the ball back I'd find a stick and throw that and when she got that I'd find anything else, absolutely confusing the thing to bits. It was hilarious. I could have played these game for hours. In fact, I think sometimes I actually did to the point where it was getting dark. But Holly enjoyed it and, hey, I was keeping the bitch fit. Other times I would wind the dog up by throwing the ball back and forward with me mates over the living room and watching her dart back and forth, going absolutely mental, barking and growling. Holly used to hate it when I ran away from her and she would chase after me. We had a wooden gloss floor in the kitchen, so I used to make Holly sit at the far end away from the door, ask her to stay, then I'd run fast as I could, with Holly slipping on the floor trying to catch me but getting nowhere, just falling over and slipping. It was so fucking funny.

We had really lovely neighbours – after all, as I'd find out later, everybody needs good neighbours! – who would pop round every so often for drinks. There were also a couple of lads that I would knock around with on the estate from time to time and get up to mischief with. Next door lived a lovely old woman who got on so well with Holly especially that when we eventually moved on to another house years later, I gave her the dog as they were both old by then and the woman next door needed the company.

Most of the time, however, I actually enjoyed me own company. I didn't need pals to make me feel adventurous. I was quite capable of using me imagination. Cos I couldn't sit still half the time anyways, I would dream about crazy ideas to keep me occupied. Ideas that were often actually more dangerous than I anticipated! For this though, I'd usually wait for Dad to head back offshore, as I knew he would only tell me off. Then, as soon as he left, I would start going berserk with all sorts of mischief!

For example, thinking I was some kind of SAS badman, or Arnold Schwarzenegger in *Commando*, I dragged some clean sheets out of an airing cupboard and tried to turn them into parachutes. I managed to climb onto the roof of the bungalow, gathered the four corners of the sheet in me hands and stepped towards the edge of the roof. There, without a thought in the world, I prepared for me heroic jump. 1 ... 2 ... 3 ... off he goes over the edge. But instead of gently reaching the ground ten-or-so-feet below me, as you'd expect someone using a parachute would do, I just fucking plunged straight down with nee 'parachute' support at all and just hit the ground with a full-on thump. The result? I sprained me ankle and got a stern telling off.

Having not learnt me lesson from that particular silly exercise, I then came up with another lethal idea of trying to make a zip line that would stretch from one of the conifer trees at the end of the garden to the highest point on the roof of the house. Having tied one end of some climbing rope around one of the tree trunks and the other end tied to some fucking light fixture at the very top point of the bungalow roof, I launched meself onto the 'wire'. But no sooner had I left me perch when the 'wire' just sagged suddenly as the tree at the end of the garden bent dangerously sideways! Once again I hit the ground and almost broke me legs, man.

Having learnt that I was never going to be able to turn the garden into a military assault course, I decided to do what most bored little boys do – torture poor animals. Don't worry! I didn't try to microwave a cat or anything (that's just shocking). Nee, I'm talking about hoying bricks at hornets' and wasps' nests that were wedged in the top corner of me back garden shed and in the wall in the front garden between the bungalow and the garage. See, I was a propa little shit.

The thing is, I was an adventurous kid. I loved climbing and I literally had no real sense of danger. So when I was heaving meself up on to the roof and jumping around the garden like a squirrel, me mam was beside herself with worry in case I'd got hurt and she'd scream and yell at me to calm down, but I'd just blank her and crack on. Dad on the other hand, if he was home, would be going fucking nuts.

If he caught me running around on the roof, he'd tell me to get down now and give me a swift clip across the lugs.

But I wasn't always a little bastard – at least I don't think I was! I had some good points too. For one – and this might come as a shock to you too – I was pretty good around the house cos I was a little OCD.

When I had a shower I had to do it in a certain way. Once I found a new love for keeping clean I'd order it like this: shampoo in me hair first, then rinse it off, then add the conditioner, leave it in, then apply the body wash with one of them fucking fluffy sponge things, before rinsing that off, getting some face scrub on, washing that off with warm water before going cold for the last few minutes, rinsing out the conditioner and tightening me pores. I did it every time. And I still do.

I was also obsessed with washing me hands constantly. In fact, at me first school I used to wash me hands so much that I ended up with really dry skin on me hands. I just couldn't live with dirty hands so I just had to keep washing them all the time. If I touched something outside like dust or a grubby bin bag, then I'd have to nash to a sink and scrub me hands to bits. I was just obsessed with it, like.

Although I hated the process of washing up, I was pretty happy to help dry the dishes, and if I saw crumbs on the floor then I would get the vacuum cleaner out and kick off with the vacuuming, going all over the house just after finding a few crumbs somewhere. I would be really thorough and used all the attachments to make sure the skirting boards and all the little crevices were spotless. Then I'd actually move the bed and do underneath it. What a complete geek I was!

Just the thought of there being any dust or crumbs lying about the place would propa freak me out. Something in me heed would tell me the place had to be propa spotless, otherwise it would just do me head in and make me more angry. In fact, I would wipe the skirting boards with dusters, dust the top of the cupboards, wipe the light fixtures and even clean the fucking duster after. I loved the duster, like, and as you'll find out later I became bit of a pro duster meself (if you get what I mean!). I would do everything, cleaning-wise. I'd empty me drawers and cupboards, give them a clean with bleach wipes and polish and put them back again, refilled and organised neatly. I couldn't stop until the whole room had been done, like. It sounds crackers, but I had to do it. It was compulsory in me mind, haha!

While I was obsessed with keeping things propa tidy, I also had a habit of hoarding shit too. I just couldn't let go of anything, just in case I ever needed it again. Even now I am a little bit like that . . . I mean, I have so many clothes in me new flat that if I were to lay out all me T-shirts, for example, I reckon they would probably stretch as long as five football pitches. Nee joke, it's daft!

Thinking about it, I must have been a right little bastard to live with, me. So, sorry Mam and Dad. If I lost a piece of Lego I would go mad cos I liked everything to be in order. Unlike most kids, whenever I would finish playing with it, I would put it all back carefully in the box so I knew that every piece had been returned to its rightful place even if I did smash it up most of the time.

Meanwhile, at school me behaviour was similar. When I was propa agitated I would just constantly stab me school book with me pen, pure scribing it in half. If someone was holding a book up I would stick me pen right through it, or I would go up to a mate and grab his jotter and just rip it in half. It was a propa laugh!

I remember one time at school, me class made these papier mâché bowls. When we had finished them, I went round and pure crushed everyone's and messed them up. Just. For. Fun! What a fucking wanker, eh? Some kids in the class even start crying man, I was like, 'Here, it's papier mâché man! Calm doon!'

I didn't know what was wrong with me, like, but I was enjoying meself, haha. I could be just sitting somewhere, or walking around and then I would feel compelled to do something stupid. I used to have this Thomas the Tank Engine lunch box which was totally battered. I'd take me sandwiches out and then I would kick the shit out of the thing all over the yard, using it as a football. I would actually put it on the ground and take a run and kick the fucker. I knew what I was doing was norty and a bit daft – the teachers made that very clear to me indeed – but I never thought there was something odd going on.

Me mam, on the other hand, was beginning to suspect that not all was right with me. No, she didn't think I was possessed by the devil like fucking Damien from *The Omen*; instead at first she thought I was deaf, cos I didn't listen to no one!

MAM: I used to tell our Scott to do things, like put his socks on in the morning. Then I'd come back to him about ten minutes later and he still hadn't put his socks on. And I would say, 'Come on Scott, put your socks on', and he'd say 'Yeah, yeah.' I remember I said to Rob one time, 'Do you think he's a bit deaf?' and he barked back at me, 'No!' But I knew there was something not quite right, even if me husband didn't think so.

So Mam at least knew there was a problem. But Dad didn't really understand and we didn't really get on all that well at this point in time. We were just always arguing. Mam would tell me to do something and I wouldn't listen. Me concentration was shit and I would get bored so easily and always got really argumentative as well – I would argue to the death about anything just cos I could.

I think me mam must have been getting to the end of her tether. As each day passed, I was becoming more and more difficult to manage. But she was beginning to think that me erratic behaviour was more than me just being disobedient. Even though Dad didn't agree with her, and was convinced I was simply a misbehaving little rascal who just needed a stern telling off once in a while, she was convinced there was another reason why I was such a difficult little fella, so what was up with me? Why was I being a Scotty terror?

Me mam was beginning to suspect that not all was right with me.

51

One day, Mam received a phone call that came out of the blue but helped explain everything. Basically, the answer landed in her lap. Now cos this part of me life is nothing but a blur, once again, I'm going to pass you over to me mam! Crack on, Mam!

MAM: Me mam rang me and she says, 'I've watched this programme on the telly last night, about this doctor treating a boy whose behaviour fits Scott to a tee.' Eventually I tracked this guy down to a uni in Bristol and gave him a call. He was a very understanding man and listened to me intently as I gave him an overview of Scott's behaviour, punctuating what I said with the occasional 'ah-ha', 'yes' and 'yes, I see!' When I was done, he told me that what I'd described are classic symptoms of ADHD.

He went on to explain that the symptoms include a difficulty in staying focused or paying attention, an inability to control behaviour, and hyperactivity. It was like checking off a list of what Scott is like. I'd never heard of this condition before, but part of me was feeling over the moon cos finally someone was telling me that me Scott wasn't just a norty boy, but someone with a problem that he simply couldn't control. When we met with the doctor he did some tests, and afterwards he said to us, 'Look, I have something he can take.' It was something called Ritalin. He told me, 'ADHD is a lack of dopamine in the brain which controls impulsiveness and concentration. By taking Ritalin, this ups its level.'

52

What I can remember from back then is that Dr McArdle was an absolute diamond who reminded me for some reason of Pierce Brosnan. He was a patient and very knowledgeable man and he really listened to what I had to say, which when you're so young is just perfect, like. When I started taking Ritalin, I began to notice immediate changes in me behaviour and I could definitely sense that me attention span was getting better.

I saw Dr McArdle several times and I think he was a pretty canny man who could see what was going on in me life, even if I didn't realise it meself. I remember on one visit, he took me to one side and asked me some questions about me home life. I'm not sure why, but now I look back, perhaps he had sensed something wasn't right at home and he was trying to work out if any of me behaviour was in some way related to that. Now I'm an adult, I'd be interested to know what his views would be these days and would love to speak to him again, so if you're reading this McArdle, then gizza shout, mate!

So Mam and Dad were happy that their wayward son was finally under some control. But, truth be told, while I may have appeared to have calmed down a lot, I was still a propa norty kid. I still liked to knock about and cause trouble, stick people up and do all the things I used to do. But it was when I headed off to middle school, where I really started coming out of me shell, meeting me best friends in the world, and becoming the daft cunt you all know and love today!

7

THE FOUR HORSEMEN OF
THE APOCALYPSE

Middle school was the first day of the rest of me life. Richard Coates Church of England School would be the place to be, where I would meet probably the best friends a boy could make.

Although I was certainly not nervous at all about starting a new school (by aged nine, me confidence was through the fucking roof), I was conscious of the fact that I wouldn't really nah many people there at all. Me best pals at the time, Sam, Alex and Adam, had all decided to go from Gossy first school to Gossy middle. So, for me this first day was me way of gauging what the next few years would be like, and how much mayhem I was gunna cause.

The school was totally unlike the previous ones I'd been to. It was propa massive, very modern and had its own athletics pitch complete with basketball courts, running tracks and long jump pits etc. It all felt very grown up, like!

Sitting in me first form room, I looked around to see if there was anyone there who looked worthy of being me mate or was me type of person. At first glance I wasn't sure at all, but hey, how could I tell at such an early stage?

With everyone sitting silent at their tables, the teacher – for the life of me I can't remember who it was – was running through all the formalities of school. Boring shite. Of course, me mind started to wander, not cos of me ADHD, but cos what was coming out of the teacher's mouth bored me to death.

I could see that the rest of the kids were feeling the same as me and I swear I saw a couple of them actually nod off at their desks. I knew I had to do something to liven everyone up. So when Teach asked us all if we'd found our lockers okay, I took me chance and called out, 'Yeah, sir, but there's a fucking rat in mine, mate.'

I don't actually know why I said that, haha – it was just the first radge thing that popped in me head. Nevertheless, after a hesitant pause, the classroom erupted into laughter and everyone turned around to stare at the joker in the class-room – me. One of the boys was a guy I would discover was called Michael. He was a small guy with light hair and he looked shy and thin, and not the type to get up to nee good (but boy was I wrong there).

Someone else who caught me eye was a lad called Benjie, who I noticed almost immediately had the same kind of wicked glint in his eye as I did. In that split second, I could tell that we were cut from the same cloth. In fact, I think right there and then we'd set each other an unspoken challenge to find out which of the two of us was the most outrageous. Here Benjie remembers how we became pals.

BENJIE: I think we became friends cos we were competing for attention in class. We were always trying to outdo each other. When I saw him for the first time, I knew that me and Scotty were similar and from that moment on we would bring the worst out in each other. When he'd start trouble, so did I, only I'd do something bigger and better. We'd both get sent out of the classroom for being disruptive or asking really stupid questions as we'd get together and cause trouble. People found what we did funny so we really played up to it. I remember our first joint attack took place not long after we started at the same school. There was a stairway that goes down three or four steps from the corridor and we had a bag of ink cartridges and made a mural on the ceiling with ink. We got caught cos the teachers came out and saw us doing it.

And here's how Michael remembers that first encounter.

MICHAEL: I remember the first day when the teacher asked, 'Is everyone all right, did you find your lockers okay?' And then this kid piped up behind me and said, 'Well, there's a fucking rat in me locker.' I looked over and it was Scott. He's always been quite radge. I was a lot shyer at that point so I wouldn't have immediately become friends with him. But I think we accidentally became friends. Ha!

But it wasn't just the three of us in the group. Our gang had other members, such as Chad, who I had sat next to in class on me first day. He was a chubby, stocky lad with a full-on baby face, but he was fucking ruthless: not really as stupid, but just mad! He was classed by some as the hardest kid in the year cos he really didn't give a shit and used to get in fights all the time (and win). And yet, there was something about him that I really liked and he fast became one of me best mates.

Although we were all up for a bit of havoc, I think Chad was probably more disruptive than Benjie and me and I think he had more of a serious chip on his shoulder regarding authority. You see, while Benjie and I would back down if a teacher was on our case, Chad would have nee problem about standing up to the teacher and trying to shout them down. And if they dared try to punish him – well, he was just not having it.

We're not sure where he got this hard edge from, but we knew that his dad was propa nails, propa radge, and worked on the rigs like mine did. But even though he sounds like a maniac, he was a good mate who would just take things a little bit too far! In fact, later on in high school, after we had drifted apart, we heard that Chad had allegedly got expelled after holding up a bus driver with a BB gun. The bus driver thought it was a real gun and shat himself, haha!

Another lad in our crew was called Marcus. Again, he was cut from the same cloth as us. Funny, good at football, but a fella who often got quite angry. He might have seemed a bit of a head case to the rest of the school, but by the end of middle school we had become very close friends indeed.

You see, the thing with us lunatics was, while we may have been perceived by many as badly behaved tearaways, underneath the bravado we were genuinely nice lads. We were just young lads messing around.

I mean, if we saw someone being bullied we'd step in straight away to protect them, cos we didn't agree with anything like that. We might have been mad and radge, but we had morals and good hearts. Our 'problem' was with authority. Actually, no, that's not right. For someone like Chad, I think that was the case. But for Benjie and me, we just wanted to have a laugh, and enjoy ourselves as much as possible, without ever hurting anyone.

Underneath the bravado we were genuinely nice lads.

While it was clear that Chad and Benjie and I were offsprings of the devil, the school was a Church of England one, where prayers were said in assembly. Although nowhere near as strict as me first school, teachers were keen to stamp out bad behaviour and were pretty free in dishing out punishments.

In most schools, if you got in trouble, you'd probably end up getting a detention after school or maybe have to write a hundred lines. But at Richard Coates Church of England School they also had this thing called isolation. So if you were norty, they would separate you from your pals and make you stand somewhere all by yourself in a corridor or summat.

So sometimes at lunchtime we would have to stand in corners of the lunch hall as a punishment, while people just walked past and cracked on with their food. I remember one day Benjie was ordered to stand behind the music stage while another mate – Chad I think – was put down the end of a corridor next to the indoor sports hall. Where I was positioned I could see Chad along the corridor quite clearly and when no one in authority was looking I whipped out some pennies and launched them down the corridor at him. The next thing we heard was the thunderous crashing and banging of drum kits falling over. It turns out that Benjie had got bored of just standing there behind the music stage on his own and had decided to chuck some stuff around instead. The headmaster was propa foaming.

In spite of me taking Ritalin, I was still easily distracted and of course, trouble was never far away. As many of you know, morning assemblies can be pretty dim experiences. Sitting on a hard wooden floor having to sing hymns and that, all you got was numb arse cheeks, so how can you blame us for getting bored. Most of the time I'd be sat behind a bird – swell – so I'd just direct me attention to staring at her the whole time instead of signing along with the hymns. One particular morning I started chatting with one of the girls along the row. All of a sudden a voice boomed, 'Scott – get up!' I pure jumped out of me skin, looked up and the head teacher on the stage who was looking down at me, giving me a propa evil eye. He ordered me to stand up in front of everyone in the year and face the wall at the front of the assembly. Me face literally went bright pink, haha. I reluctantly dragged me feet up on to the stage and faced the wall. I was so embarrassed I was actually shaking. Absolute liberty for me!!

Eventually the teachers cottoned on to the fact that Chad, Benjie and I brought out the worst in each other and we were cruelly separated (we'd been in the same class) and put into different classes to keep us apart! Good idea, or should I say nice try. Don't underestimate us boys. While we may have been forced apart, that didn't stop us from causing bedlam together in school. What we had to do now was to form a plan of action and decide at what time we would cause trouble together. Which meant we pre-arranged a time to start going mad so that we would be kicked out of classroom and made to stand outside at roughly the same time. Once free of the lessons, we'd run around the corridors causing havoc, kicking over lockers or finding things to smash to smithereens, such as roof tiles. Once we got made to stand in a room together quietly which was stupid, as we went a bit mad with poor Mr Clogg's model ship.

Mr Clogg was the good-natured woodwork teacher who loved building shit. One of his treasured creations was this wooden replica of a ship that must have taken him about a hundred hours to build. It was actually pretty impressive as it goes. Really intricate and you could tell that a real craftsman had put it together. But that meant nowt when me and me mates were on the rampage. So us three being isolated in the technology room was a disaster. Now, I'm not going to say which one of us actually did it (we've all moved on now, with propa jobs and that!), but one of us took that magnificent ship out of the woodwork cupboard, gently put it on the floor and started wheeling it along, then all of a sudden started propa stamping on it. It was absolutely fucked and in tiny pieces. It was hilarious, especially as when Mr Clogg happened to stroll into the room one of us tried to stuff it back in the cupboard. I was in hysterics watching. (Oops, I guess that narrows it down to not being me, so a guess it was between the other two lads ... cough cough 'Benjie' cough!) Looking back now, we were right arseholes. And yeah, that was a pretty shitty thing to do. But at the time, we were stupid boys and we found it class impressing each other with daft pranks. Mr Clogg, I know we said it at the time, but we're sorry again, haha!! It's funny cos I'm actually good mates with his son now, Jackson Clogg, who is a few years younger and I always ask how his dad is and would love to see him again to find out just how bad we really were. So, Mr Clogg, if you're reading this invite me round for dinner mate! (He's probably thinking 'fucking no chance'.)

After school we'd usually hang around the school field to play football, but it wasn't too long before we'd get tired of the game and end up running around on the roof of the school where loads of lost balls ended up. The school caretaker lived on the grounds so it was always funny getting chased by him. He would be furious with us and constantly running after us (he was a bit like that Scottish bloke off *The Simpsons*, groundskeeper Willie!). You can see how we drove the school staff insane all the time. Looking back, I get about a million stories through me head about the stuff we did. I almost feel sorry for them!

Our behaviour was so bad that eventually the school could do nothing else with us and eventually one of our group was expelled. Although in reality what happened to him was pretty out of order.

Again, I don't wanna say which one of us it was, but he had been put in isolation yet again. And, once again, he had started lunging stuff around cos he was pissed off. To deal with this, the teachers thought it wasn't cruel in the slightest to lock him in a dark cupboard where the chairs are all stacked for a couple of hours. Eventually, after the monotony of the dark cupboard got too much, he broke out and ended up running home to tell his dad that he had been locked against his will in a cupboard. Bad crack!

But even though his father accused the school of punishing his son in a cruel way, the head said that this particular incident was merely the last straw and told him – as there were just a few weeks left of the final term of middle school – that there was nee point in coming back.

So, all in all, we were right divvies and eventually our bad behaviour would get us into some very serious trouble. But more of those stories laterz . . .

8

'What Am I Gunna Do about Me Skinny Legs?'

Middle school was definitely a time of great transition and transformation for me.

When I was around ten, I'd had a sudden growth spurt, which elongated me body, so I was actually pretty tall for me age, which I was happy about, cos no one really wants to be a midget, do they?! Then puberty kicked clean in and me body began to go through the usual changes: shoulders filling out, pubes coming through, and me chod was kicking off, oi oi! During this time I was starting to become a little more self-conscious about girls than before and wanted to look me best so I could catch their eyes.

Now, I was never what you'd exactly call fat, me, just very slightly chubby in parts. Apart from that I was actually quite lean as I really loved playing sports at school, but me body never really had any definition in the way, say, an Olympian or a footballer's had.

But still, I wasn't very happy about me body. There were bits of it that just weren't the way I wanted them to be. So distraught about it was I in me middle-school years that I even bent me mam's ear about it – after all, mams know everything, don't they?

'Mam, look at me skinny legs,' I said. 'What am I gunna to do about them? I look like a fucking sparrow.'

'I'm not sure you can do much,' Mam said, looking me up and down, and then staring long and hard at me ostrich legs. 'You've got good long legs, they're never going to be like Tizer bottles or rugby balls. If you were a short-arse they'd probably bulk up more, but you're not so deal with it!'

Well aye Mam, cheers! That's just what I needed to hear. Well, I wasn't taking no for an answer. I wanted to have a body I was proud of so I got motivated and tried to do something about it.

Coincidentally, I had recently become mates with a guy called Lloyd. He was this bulky ripped kid who used to like getting naked all the time. (I guess if you had a body like his it was nee botha – busting pecs, six pack, barely an ounce of fat on the kid – then that's exactly what you would do too.) Anyway, I got chatting to him and he got me started in the gym and we became really good mates.

Me new look was propa catching girls' eyes.

Over the next few months I embarked on a ridiculously strict fitness and nutrition regime. I went to the gym five or six times a week, where I would go on the running machine every single day for like an hour religiously, until I trimmed up and lost the extra fat. Then I started lifting weights about. Eventually I started looking lethal, quite big and me new look was propa catching girls' eyes.

As I continued to get fitter and fitter, I began to get more involved in school athletics, which I have to admit I was pretty good at anyways. In fact, me love for sport led me to attend summer school one year where I played softball, ran huge obstacle courses, took part in fencing, tennis tournaments and even fucking archery, as well as trying out various athletic events. Sadly, I threw it all away by getting meself chucked off the summer course when I was caught stealing money and ice pops from the shop on CCTV. I was propa humiliated.

But that daft time didn't dampen me interest in sport and most years I practically ruled the school's annual sports days.

Normally, kids in each of the four class teams throughout middle school would take part in just three events on the day as that was the standard requirement, but cos I was so exceptional at various sports such as javelin, discus, long jump, high jump and so on, and track events such as the 100m sprint and finishing position in the relays, me sports teacher told me he wanted to enter me into 12 events cos, he confided in me, pretty much no one else was good enough in the class, apart from two lads, Dan Johnson and me top mate Michael Carr. Twelve though! Can you believe that man? It was unheard of and of course I was propa chuffed.

Me, Benjie and Dan were the best at sport out of the whole year and, thanks to me teacher's huge belief in me, I was walking around the sports field with full-on swagger, confident in me ability.

When it came to the events, I did meself proud, like. I wasn't nervous cos I knew I was capable of smashing it. In the end, I came first in triple jump, second in long jump, first in shotput, and I broke the school record for discus, javelin and high jump. Relay, I came second, then I won the 400m and came second in the 200m, along with near top in the others. Not bad going for a guy who was barely off the field all day.

A while later, cos of our success, Benjie, Dan and I were entered into a county-wide sports day against other schools. If I'm honest, me heart wasn't really in the event and we got there and spent most of our time knocking about at a neighbouring antiques fair, instead of actually preparing for the event.

Then when it came to the competition, I really let meself down. During the discus event, for example, I propa fucked up the first two throws and me third wasn't great either. I ended up coming third which was a liberty for me cos I knew for a fact I could have won. And when we took part in the javelin event, we discovered that the javelins we were using were way heavier than the ones we'd been using in training. Unsurprisingly, we came home pretty much empty-handed. Gutted!

When I wasn't being a sporty kid I went through a weird and very short-lived period as a hippy/goth-skateboarder guy. How mad is that? Now, for the life of me, this brief moment in time remains just a very vague memory. I mean,

I have occasional flashbacks to a time when I wore a lot of black rock band T-shirts and The Offspring or Metallica hoodies, but can't actually recall any specifics about what I did or where I went. But I know it definitely happened cos Benjie and Michael remember quite a lot to this day, and still have me life about it. All they can say about this particularly ill-advised period is that I grew me hair a bit longer and started to dress differently but can't recall who the hell I was actually hanging out with at the time, which would lead me to think that it was all part of our collective imaginations, but the boys do remember these vague details. Here you go:

BENJIE: I couldn't tell you anything about the people Scott hung around with, but they were all similar in dress. He used to wear Slipknot T-shirts with black flared trousers. I'm very sure he also used to paint his nails black, or did, that is, until his old mates took the piss out of him. All in good nature of course . . . what a geek!

MICHAEL: I can't really remember their names either, but Scott still kept his normal group of friends as well as mixing with this new group. To be honest, he didn't change much really apart from listening to music like The Offspring, Linkin Park and Blink 182.

As I said, that hippy-drip period of me life was very short-lived indeed and it wasn't long before I started turning meself into the man/charver I am today.

9

SCOTT AND THE BOYS START GOING RADGE!

If you thought we were terrors at school, you ain't seen nothing yet. As we approached our teen years, we did what most boys our age did – cause trouble on the streets, get drunk and try to get with girls.

When you're about 11, 12 or 13, options for entertaining yourselves were limited. We looked way too young to blag our way in to bars, youth clubs were boring and hanging out at shopping malls like Eldon Square and the Metrocentre was fun for a bit but got boring after a while. So it was up to us to make our own fun. And I'm telling you now, that's exactly what we did.

Me and me boys, Benjie and Michael, and the rest of the lads were pretty adventurous tykes at this point, and would go and hang out down by the Ponteland river (the river Pont, it's called) where we would make Tarzan swings so that we could hilariously hurl ourselves across the river. The point where we made the swings was at the back of this graveyard. It really was a mint crack. It was a simple, cheap activity and it kept us entertained for hours. See what a length of rope can do for a bunch of bored lads? At least we weren't tying each other up!

Of course, we also loved that there was a massive element of danger to all this rope shite. This was nee activity for pussies, this was as masculine as you could get. We felt like real-life gorillas: we'd grab these ropes tied to some propa old oak tree hanging high up over this river, then we'd run from left to right or vice versa, run as hard as we could to the other side and straight off the edge. We would get about nine seconds of air-time, man, before having to land properly back on the ground without sliding back down the river banks.

The fun part of this oh-so-simple game was that we got to live out our dreams of daring, seeing how far we could push each other to do mad stunts. And every time we launched ourselves across the river, we felt like nothing could stop us. Unless, of course, we let go of the rope on purpose to try to make it across to the other side (which never ended well) or we slipped and fell into the rocky water below.

I have to admit, as a bit of a sportsman, I was pretty good at it as it goes and rarely fell off at all. Sometimes I even hooked me legs up over the piece of wood and swung around upside down – now that was radge. But of course, it was hilarious when some of the boys couldn't make it across or when the rope snapped! It was fucking hilarious! We would be creased up every time someone full-on planted in the river.

Benjie was a dab hand at swinging too, but even he had a few mishaps. There was this one time that he really cracked us up. As he prepared himself to jump, he made sure that he had wrapped his hands around the rope tightly enough before launching himself across the river. Then he was off! All looked good to start with. As he whooshed through the air like Tarzan he looked like he was going to clear the river. But just before he made it over to the other side, he suddenly lost his grip, slipped and fell face first onto the river bank that was covered in rocks. Luckily, he walked away in one piece with just a few bruises – but then me Benjie is one tough kid and a scrape like this meant nowt to him. But watching him go down like a sack of shit was just fantastic. If only we'd been filming it, we could have made £250 from *You've Been Framed*, man. Funny thing with this story was that we actually hopped over the fence at the back of the field like we did most lunchtimes, as the food in school was shite, so we would go to the chippy then to the Tarzan swing. Benjie had this fall during lunch break so all his uniform was propa soaked through to the max, we had to quickly nash to me nan and granddad's house as they lived nearby, so he could borrow a white shirt before getting back for lessons. Me granddad wasn't even bothered, as I told him we had a sports training day and he fell in the swimming pool (there wasn't even a pool at the school and he was covered in mud, haha). I'm sure me granddad knew what we were up to but he just played along and told us to hurry back to school.

It was at this early age that we started to get into booze,

along with the other bad traits like skipping lessons and bailing out of school grounds to go get food. But isn't that what every young boy does? It's a rite of passage, right? While money was never really a problem, as me dad would always give me a good wedge of pocket money and I used to make a fortune hustling kids at school with Pokémon cards, the fact most of us looked too young to go into a shop and pass as 18 meant that booze was hard for us to get hold of. Which meant that we had to beg and plead with someone like Marcus or Benjie's older radge brothers to stock us up, which they did – for a price.

We also had a mate called Jason – who we nicknamed Urg. He was a tall monster of a bloke who started growing a beard at, like, fucking 12. He looked way older than his years. In fact, he would constantly get turned away from an under-18s night cos the people on the door thought he was in his 20s and was just there being a bit of a weirdo. While Jason might not have appreciated nature's gift of looking older as a kid, for the rest of us we were buzzing as hardly anyone bothered to ask him for ID. We took full advantage of this!

Once we'd got our hands on the peeve, we'd go sit in the park next to the high school or in the kids' park at these tiny little tables that were designed for kids a lot smaller than us. We felt like such hard men as we sat there necking cans of Carling or a big 3-litre bottle of Scrumpy Jack cider. Cos we weren't used to alcohol in these early days we'd quickly get propa smashed and then we'd be rolling around the place like complete idiots. As time went on, we moved on to spirits and I have this vivid memory of Michael swigging vodka out of the bottle – he used to stash a quarter-litre bottle in his back pocket.

But even though we were brazenly drinking in the open air we still had to be cautious about who would see us cos the local police in Ponteland were pretty vigilant and if they saw us necking booze they'd be on our tail in a second, always chasing us. We were always getting watched by the local police cos they'd see a big group of us knocking around the streets causing bother, but we knew the streets really well and would always lose them by running along this dirt track we knew that ran for five miles through the housing estates in Darras Hall, which was a neighbouring area that merged into Ponteland, all the way to the airport runways. Normally we would manage to outrun the police as they were usually quite out of shape and couldn't be bothered to chase us, but sometimes one of us would get caught and be given a caution, telling off or sent home. Good crack! Getting chases off the police was propa thrilling as you will find out later. It was pretty much a day-to-day thing for our group!

During the week, me and the boys would meet up late at night for what we liked to call midnight missions – which basically meant roaming the streets causing havoc at night-time and sleeping on the streets or in a fucking bush!

One night, full of drink and looking for trouble, we decided to go on a garden hopping midnight mission in Darras Hall. This basically involved us lot rampaging through people's gardens while they're tucked up in bed asleep. It was an absolute frisk. The gardens in Darras Hall were all massive (you could call it the rich part of Newcastle), streets full of mansions and houses like castles. In one garden, as we were all hopping fences and running around like lunatics in a big fuck-off group we came across this massive trampoline. Of course, we couldn't resist having a few bounces on it ... all 10–15 of us – well, it would be stupid not to wouldn't it – but then one of us came up with the genius idea of rolling it out the back garden onto the main road. What we were going to do with it when it got there was anyone's guess. But we just did it anyway. As it was so big it took a canny few of us to roll it out without waking up any of the neighbours or the people who owned the house.

When we got it to the street, we just whacked it bang in the middle of the road and stood back to admire our work – amazing! And that was it. Brilliant, aye? I mean, what else would we do with it, like, except perhaps start bouncing on the thing again? We had a propa laugh with it and started going mental turning it on its side and running into it full force to see what happens. This was a wicked crack – a bunch of lads at 3 a.m. going mad in the streets with a giant trampoline – but before we knew it, down the long streets of Runnymede Road in Darras Hall we could see blue flashing lights ... nightmare!! We never knew whether someone had called them or they were just doing their routine patrol because it wasn't the first time we'd done stuff like this.

'Fucking police ... NASH!!' Shouting this, no one hung round, and everyone just literally scattered in all different directions, a few of the lads through one garden, a few through another and so on. I took off with Lloyd and ended up losing him in some garden, then jumped a few more fences before hiding behind a rock in a front garden right next to the main road where the police drove up. I literally was lying there for what felt like hours as the police were going up and down the street shining torches through the hedges in each driveway including the one I was hiding in. I must have been there a long time, like, cos the next thing I remember I was being rudely awoken at about 7 a.m. by a barking dog and a woman who was shouting, 'What the hell are you doing here?' Still pissed, I just got up and took off, walking back home in broad daylight covered in pieces of shrub and mud from all the gardens I'd been bopping through! It was like a walk of shame, only without the shag, GUTTER!

I found out the next day, once I spoke to the lads, that Marcus and a few others had been chased through a garden by the pigs and they hopped this fence, landing face-first in a huge deep pond, getting absolutely drenched but managing to get away. Benjie, Michael and a few others had gone in another direction and Benjie had ran into and collapsed a 100-metre-long fence. Mine wasn't as fun though, as I basically just slept behind a rock in someone's drive. It's funny actually, cos years later I discovered that the house we'd nicked the trampoline from actually belonged to a mate of ours, and the garden I slept in was one of me later best pal's, haha! That night we were so pissed we didn't know where we were.

Moving on to another adventure during our school days, the industrial estate in Ponteland was home to this pure massive derelict factory called Dobson's Sweet Factory. In years gone by it had produced many of the sweets that kids around the country had grown up eating and rotted their teeth away with. Sadly, as with many businesses those days, the factory had closed down some years before and the building was left alone to rot, just like our teeth. Which meant me and the boys had yet another ideal location to cause havoc.

I remember the first time we went to explore it I was totally creeped out by it cos it looked like one of those old decrepit buildings you see in horror films. To actually get near the building was a challenge in itself. First you had to slip through a fence around the back of the building, then heave yourself over a wall, go through a broken part in another fence, then there was a metal panel on the back door you could lift up for people as they crawled in. Over the years the police had tried to find many ways of securing the place to keep people like us out, but someone would always find a way to get back in.

When we finally made it inside that first time, we were mesmerised by the size of the cavernous great hall. It was ridiculously huge and looked like that secret room in the *Batman* films – in the Wayne skyscraper. This was as long and as wide as a basketball court and the roof was as high as a church, with white flooring like a posh car park. Most of the machinery that was used to produce the sweets had been removed and all that remained was this rusty forklift that sadly didn't work and a massive crate that used to contain the sweets that were produced there.

As the place had been derelict for a few years or so, it was a popular hangout for lads around Ponteland who – back in the day – used to grab loads of past-their-sell-by-date sweets and sell them on to kids at school. I'm sure I bought some!

At the back of the humungous hall were a set of doors and a dark stairway that led to loads and loads of different rooms. In one of them we rifled through filing cabinets, the lot, and ended up finding huge bunches of keys in a set of drawers and proceeded to race around the whole building unlocking even more rooms and causing mayhem. Like hurricanes we raced from one to another, pulling the fluorescent lights off the ceiling and smashing them off each other and against any surface we could. We found it funny cos all this white powder shit would come out and go all over your clothes. I even got someone to smash one off me head for the laugh – I had a beanie hat on, though I got dust in me eyes and nearly choked!

Name one lad who doesn't love to smash stuff up.

We'd overturn all these filing cabinets and watch clouds of dust fill the air. If there was a window that had its glass intact we'd smash it to smithereens. We were right little bastard vandals. But it was so much fun, you nah! Name one lad who doesn't love to smash stuff up . . . exactly! It was such a mint way of releasing all that built-up frustration we had from boredom and lack of sex. I suppose without even knowing we had sexual frustration, our group must have experienced this on a daily basis at school.

When we weren't smashing the fuck out of the place, we would tell our parents that we were staying at each other's houses again and simply camp out for the night in one of the offices, where we'd spend our time playing games, necking drink and smoking buckets. This is basically a homemade hash bong, or as we liked to call it ... Tac! What it was, was using two plastic drinks bottles cut in half, you'd fill the bottom half with water and use the top half as a chillum or gauze-like thing to crumble the hash onto to light. We'd then burn the tac and put the half bottle up out the water thus being left with smoke – how fucking *Blue Peter* of us. We used to have such a buzz, running around creasing our faces off cos we were so stoned. It was wicked! As time went on we'd still hit up the factory, and end up bringing loads of people to Dobson's, even girls. Everyone was wanting in on the place. We would all meet there on weekends and get absolutely smashed or stoned and most occasions everyone would sleep there. I'd be getting right amounts of fingering girls left, right and centre in the different rooms, or getting a cheeky blowy off them as well, in the dark without interruption.

But for most of the time – and for some reason this never got boring – we would play manhunt. Sounds impressive, but it was just a more rugged way of describing hide and seek for boys. It was as simple as it sounds. Obviously in a place like Dobson's we were spoilt for choice for places to hide and sometimes one of us would wait so long to be found that we'd end up having a kip.

Over times the game got a bit out of hand, firstly the

manhunt would turn into a game called Letter, basically the same as manhunt but when one group found you they had to beat you until you gave up the letter (all teammates had a letter each, which made a word, and the goal was obviously to get the word), or people started taking huge shits behind doorways so when you walked into a room you would either step on it or smear it into the floor when opening doors. Why we did this, fuck knows! Most of the time this just scared people away from playing cos the last thing you wanted to do was step in shit, especially your pal's. Either way, it was a frisk, like, a propa frisk!

When we were a little bit older, after the factory was literally a shit house and we stopped going there, we tried our luck a few times in town to see if we could blag our way into the bars, cos we – well especially me – were dying to experience nightlife properly and buy some propa drinks. After the under-18s events in town we'd always change (having taken spare clothes with us), dress up bit more and make our way to the Bigg Market in Newcastle city centre – it's a pretty rough place where all the bars and clubs are clustered. But back then it was mint, streets full of the radgest people you'd ever seen, everyone outside on the cobbled street where there was music absolutely banging from every bar. It was also a time when bar security wasn't as strict as it is now so it was more than likely that we'd get let through the door, or some of us would!

Just to make sure that the lads who normally couldn't get in, like Michael and Marcus, had more of a chance, we got them to get some nifty IDs off the internet, fake driving licences and that, haha. You know, just in case anyone dared ever doubt that 12-year-old looking Michael was indeed a fully grown adult even though he wasn't. As if! But they really were the shittest things you have ever seen. Scrappy printouts covered in several layers of plastic. We thought they were the bollocks. Most of the time we got into bars as a group because me and big Jason looked a lot older, especially Jason: he literally looked about 35 by this time and he spoke with a constant moaning tone to his voice, like a granddad or Shrek. Whenever we rocked up to these bars on the Bigg Market, we'd send him in first because the doorman wouldn't look twice, then Michael (because with Jason looking so old and Michael looking so young they were less likely to suspect anything), followed by me, Benjie and the others with their IDs as well. I got away with it. Even though I was baby-faced it was me gym body that I had going on. I looked lethal. Also, I would walk right up to them with nee fear of getting knocked back and most of the time that worked. Confidence is always the key! Anyways, it was always an absolute buzz. Once we got in you can probably imagine what happened when we started dedicating our trouble to the town scene, but that's to come later.

10

THE RISE OF SCOTTY T – THE WOMANISER!

As you know from watching *Geordie Shore* and *Ex on the Beach* I am something of a master when it comes to seducing women. But even before I was famous, I had this incredible knack of getting sexy lasses to buck. I don't think I can actually put me finger on the secret to me astonishing success (I've had almost a thousand women in me time), but from what lasses have told me in the questionnaire I make them fill in after a shag (joke!), I think it's all down to me winning looks and me amazing confidence. But hard as it may seem to believe, I haven't always been this cocksure guy. There was a time when I was – how can I say – a little nervous around girls.

Me first kiss . . . Now, if you were paying attention, you'll remember that I said I was snogging a wee lass behind the building at me first school on and off. While that's true, I'm not sure I'd really call that me first kiss. When you're five years old, you don't really know what you're doing. You're just putting your lips together and that's it. Doing what you think other people do. So I would say that me first propa kiss happened several years later when I was just eight years old in the glamorous surroundings of the British Virgin Islands.

Me family and I had been flown over to the island of Tortola for the wedding of me mam's cousin, a lawyer who was marrying a film director. Clichéd as it sounds, it really was like a fantasy island paradise, the likes of which you only ever see in travel brochures and films. With the sun glowing in a rich blue, almost cloudless sky, the shimmering sea below practically pulsated with an aquamarine blue glow. The gorgeous beaches were covered in fine white sand and lined with palm trees that bobbed in a gentle breeze. Just a little way from the beach, a series of holiday cottages were dotted around a palm tree-covered hillside. It really was an unbelievable sight. And a world away from the concrete grey Toon I was used to. What a wonderful place for a first romance, eh?

The girl in question was Alix Kyle and she was the daughter of me mam's cousin's friend. She was eight too, and she was a child actress who had recently shot a small role in the thriller *A Time to Kill*, starring Matthew McConaughey and Sandra Bullock. I can't remember how we got talking but cos we were the only two kids at the wedding, I think we just naturally gravitated towards each other. She was a small and pretty little thing with lovely long blonde hair. Even though I was only eight years old I felt like I was a little bit in love with her. Our relationship was very innocent – we'd run along the beach, play hide and seek, build sandcastles, splash around in the sea or just lay in the hot sands playing Gameboy together. Sometimes, the adults would take us out snorkelling or we'd eat out at a beachside restaurant. It really was bliss.

Then one day while we were walking on the beach hand in hand, I turned to her, leaned in and kissed her. Then she kissed me back. It was mint. I felt like a propa grown-up and I felt a sudden rush sweep through me body. Now that was a kiss. We did it a couple of times and as we did we became more comfortable each time. But we were eight, so it didn't really lead to anything. Nee shag pad necessary just yet!

God, that's almost 20 years ago now and I still remember it pretty clearly, well the kiss part at least. But as they say, you always remember your first kiss! I wonder if Alix does. I haven't seen her since, but I have heard that she has been asking after us. I also hear she got really fit too. Ridiculously fit, in fact. So I must try to track her down.

Back home in Newcastle, it was pretty quiet on the girl front for a while, give or take the odd finger fumble at a bus stop. In the meantime, like any boy on that journey of sexual awakening, I satisfied meself sexually by watching porn and lots of it. In fact I couldn't watch enough of it. I had tapes stashed all over me room and sometimes I would stupidly leave them out and me dad would know what they were. Oh the shame! But he never said anything. Probably cos he wasn't so innocent either. Sometimes I'd nab these porn playing cards that he kept in his offshore kit and I'd slip up to the attic and entertain meself.

As I got a bit older, I started thinking with me knob. And, probably cos I practically fancied any girl who walked past me, me memories are pretty vague from this time so I can only remember quick bursts.

One of the first girls who caught me eye was one called Holly who was in year five with us. I used to really fancy her cos she was by far the fittest girl in the school. But she ended up getting with Benjie cos she really liked him. Lucky bastard. However, Benjie did tell me that even though they dated briefly he didn't actually fancy her, and just thought she was fit. He also said that aside from a double-date style Macca Ds, a bit of messing around and maybe a kiss, nothing much else happened. This made me feel a lot better. I also found out later that Holly had also asked Michael out, but he turned her down cos she scared him a bit! Er, Holly? What was so wrong with me?

When we were in our early teens me and the boys would go to under-18s discos, the ones that Jason would always be turned away from cos he looked too old. They were cheesy but fun nights where we'd all dance around to the latest chart hits, but the downside of course was that alcohol was not served, which doesn't help relax you when you're trying to tash on with someone.

Sometimes we tried to sneak some in or, if that didn't work, we'd have a nip of booze before we got there so we had a bit of extra pulling confidence. Once inside, me and the boys would dare each other to kiss as many of the girls as we could. I'd go mental and snog around 15 in a night. Cos I was gyming it a lot and looked good, I was popular at the time, so I'd be going mad. I loved it. But I found it easy to snog girls I didn't really fancy. I found it a lot harder if it was a girl I liked, cos there was more to lose.

One girl I do remember vividly was Victoria, a girl with massive tits from our school. She was sexy, she was gorgeous and I had really fancied her for a while. I was going through me body transformation at this point so I had filled out a bit, me guns were looking mighty fine and I had a bit of confidence too.

What I can remember is us all going to one of our school discos and all of a sudden there she was standing in the centre of the hall bathed in colourful light, her big tits look-ing extra massive in her top. She looked like an angel. A dirty one at least! She was propa sexy! Well, that's how I remember it, anyway. In real life, I can't actually remember too much, except I got chatting to her, started dancing with her and then bingo, I leaned in and snogged her. And this was like a propa snog, tongues and all. And it was mint. To sound like a wuss, me body felt all tingly and, well, you know, me dick suddenly kicked into action. I was beside meself with happiness. I finally had meself a propa girlfriend and I was in love! Result. I was chuffed.

Only this fairytale didn't quite have the happy ending I was after.

We had exchanged numbers and every so often I would message her, making it clear that I was definitely interested in seeing more of her (in particular I wanted to get me hands on those massive norks). I have to admit she wasn't the best at replying to messages and when she did they weren't exactly what you'd call chatty, though there was one where she told me she liked me and I stored it.

But then when I pushed her again and made it more blatant that I fancied her, I think I must have scared her off and she sent me a short and not sweet message back that broke me heart in two. It read: 'Look, it was just a kiss, I don't like yer!' Totally devastating. I did what we all do and read and reread the message again, trying to find a positive aspect from the text. But try as I might, I couldn't find one. She hadn't even signed off with a kiss. The bitch!

During me middle school years I used to knock around for a little bit with a couple of guys who lived in Kingston Park. They were right lads and shagged lasses all the time. Together we used to go to Whitley Bay on the metro. Cos they were a bit older, they could get their hands on booze so we'd spend our time by the coast just necking drinks.

One breezy day, we got chatting to these two charver girls who were hanging around the seafront. Me mate took a shine to one of them, the pretty one, which left me lumbered with the, er, other one. Now, I'm not being mean when I say this, but this girl looked like a pancake. She was horrible; her face was kind of flat and wide with her facial features some-where in the middle. She was not a beauty. But hey, I was a horny teenaged boy so I carried on talking to her and feed-ing her booze while me mate got with the other girl.

After a few hours of drinking we were pretty pissed and me mate suggested that we take the girls back to his place cos his parents were away. On the journey back I wondered what was going to happen. The booze had given me that extra bit of confidence. I knew we'd at least get a snog, cos the lass looked like she was gagging for it. Of course, I had nee expectations but if I got to shag her, then wow! Amazing.

When we got back to his house, he took his bird into his bedroom and he told me to take Pancake Face into his brother's. Now by this point, I'd kissed me fair share of girls, but I sensed that today might actually be the day that I went one step further and perhaps popped me cherry.

Pancake seemed really into me and was kissing me and touching me all over. I have to admit, she might not have been Victoria, but she was a great snog, she had a nice body, nice little tits, and she seemed willing to go all the way. As we rolled around on the bed, we touched each other in certain places and it became pretty clear indeed that we were both very excited about the situation.

Before long we had pulled off all our clothes and were kissing passionately and then without saying a word, I made me move and I was in! After about ten seconds I felt an almighty surge. 'Wow, that was fast,' I thought as I rolled back onto the bed. 'Was that really it?'

It would take me years to realise the true joys of intimacy and sex. But even though it had been a blink-and-you-miss-it experience, I was still fucking cock-a-hoop. I'd had sex! I was nee longer a virgin! I was a man! The man!

I was so excited I couldn't wait to tell the world – well, Michael and Benjie and the boys anyway! Still glowing, Pancake and I quickly threw our clothes back on and headed back into the front room where me mate and his girl were just emerging from his room. He could see in me eyes what had happened, but as he was a much more experienced lover than me, he flashed me a knowing smile, waved his hand under me nose, and said, 'Sniff me fingers.' Lovely.

Although I didn't really fancy Pancake we saw each other a couple of times, but mainly to fool around or hold hands or cuddle. I tried to convince meself for a while that I liked her, but I was too busy enjoying me newfound sexual identity and getting sucked off in parks by radgie girls who would be pretty easy and let you feel their fannies. There was one girl called Michelle who used to fancy us, who I used to finger at a bus stop and I remember when I was done me fingers fucking stunk. She was propa radge!

I was nee longer a virgin! I was a man! The man!

Over the next few years I fell for loads of girls and used me mam's car as a passion wagon. When Mam used to go to bed, I'd slip out of the house, jump in her car and go and pick up girls and shag them. I remember this one time, I was making out with this girl and when we started fucking, the windows of the car steamed up, just like in that scene in *Titanic*. Sometimes, I'd shoot me load all over the car and Mam would call me out to the car the next morning and ask, 'What the hell is that?' I really hope she never actually knew what it was!

During me teens I snogged a lot of girls but there were a couple of girls who really meant something to me.

One was called Lucy. When I met her I think she had a thing for a guy called Tom, but I was the one who got with her. We had a great time for a while and we were good for each other. But then I discovered that she kept a diary under her bed, so whenever she went to the toilet or to get a drink from the kitchen I'd grab the book and hastily flick through the pages to find out what she had said about me and to see if she had slagged me off.

WARNING: Never do this unless you wanna feel shit about yourself. To be honest, she never wrote really bad stuff, but I do remember reading this one bit where it said I had pissed her off and she questioned whether or not it was going to work out with me. There were other bits too where she'd say, 'I wish Scott would be a bit more like this.' I'd get pissed off about that and I'd kick off about it without letting her know I'd seen her diary, and then when I'd calmed down I would try to be more like the way she wanted me to be.

After Lucy there was another girl, who I'd prefer not to name. But she meant the world to me. I was at high school at the time and me and the boys would go to all these posh house parties where there were all these really fit girls. But there was one who just really stood out and I thought to meself, 'Wow, she is pretty fit.'

I fell for loads of girls.

We chatted, and it turned out she had an on-and-off boyfriend. But I ended up getting her number, messaged her and then started going out with her when she sacked the other guy off. This girl was just lovely. Her family was really nice and I would go round to see them all the time and sometimes hang out with her to babysit her sister and brother. She was the first serious girlfriend I had, the first one I really brought back to meet me mam. And me mam fell in love with her. In fact, I think she hoped that it would work out between us.

I'm not sure how it started to fizzle out but I remember cos I was going to the gym a lot, she started too and then she became really cautious about what she was eating and got really thin. Then I think we just drifted apart but we stayed friends. Now she's engaged to the guy she was seeing just before I met her.

11

SCOTT GETS ARRESTED

Boredom was the biggest problem in our early teens as you've read. Youth clubs weren't for our crew at all and we could only go to the pictures a certain amount of times before we got into trouble and banned from the place. So we had to dream up other, more interesting ways of entertaining ourselves. Unfortunately, many of them were pretty antisocial, well all of them!

The days of knocking round the streets getting into shit, literally every day, were the best memories. I look back now and laugh me head off. There are so many stories to tell, I should probably bring out another book just on me causing trouble as a teenager cos it was ridiculous how much we got away with. But sometimes we didn't get away with everything . . .

I remember this one time in Ponteland I was chilling with the crew in this brand-new glass bus stop minding me own business (actually I was fingering some dirty arse charver girl from up the way). During the crack I was getting bored (again), and decided to do some chin ups – most probably to show off me massive biceps to this easily pleased lass.

After a couple of pull ups, I heard this massive crack open like an earthquake out of King Kong's arsehole, followed by a huge smash and then just like in a cartoon, the whole fucking thing pure collapsed around me, shattering glass all over the place. Now, I could have made a run for it, but the bloke at the local curry house right next door had seen what I had done, called the police and wouldn't let me go until they arrived.

When the po po turned up, I recognised one of the officers as a copper we all knew in the village as 'Pinkie'. We called him that cos, well, the daft cunt looked like a big pig with a moustache like a roadsweeper. All he was missing was a snout and a curly tail!

We knew him all too well cos he was the copper who would always be passing by whenever we were getting up to nee good. It was like he had a sixth sense or something cos he'd always find us in the middle of doing stupid things. In fact, we'd see him so regularly that we'd often shout 'Pinkie' at him just to piss him off, knowing full well that the bastard couldn't catch us.

I remember one snowy winter, he caught us all drinking somewhere and started running after us. Big mistake, wey ... FOR HIM. As we were younger and fitter there was nee way he could keep up with us, like, but that didn't stop him from charging after us like a Spanish bull. However, after about two minutes, we suddenly noticed that he'd disappeared, or at least had quit chasing us. We stopped, turned back and saw that he'd slipped on this iced-over puddle and fallen flat on his fat arse – nearly caused a tectonic wave. We were all creasing and he was so pissed off, which of course made it even funnier.

Anyway, back to the bus stop. When Pinkie saw it was me, he raised his eyebrows and nodded at me in that way people do when they're not entirely surprised by what they see and then he did me for vandalism. Mam and Dad were foaming.

Another of me favourite pastimes (for you NOT to try at home) was when me and the boys stole car badges. Back in the mid- to late-90s it was nuts! It was! Really. Basically, me and a bunch of mates would run around the posher neighbourhoods, venture into people's drives and collect as many car badges as possible. The flashier the better.

After a while we had collected a good stack of them, but they weren't always easy to get. BMW were the simplest to pull off – just a quick wedge with a flat-head screwdriver – while Porsche ones were a bit harder cos they had glass in them and sometimes when you were prying away you would either bend them out of shape or crack the black and red glass. If we did either, then we'd just leave them where they were, still on the car, but propa bent!

As you'd expect, the car badge that was most sought after was the Spirit of Ecstasy hood ornament from a Rolls-Royce. Obviously, the fact that not many households in Newcastle drove round in such a sick set of wheels meant the badge was something of a rare find. When we found out that one house in the Darras Hall area had a Rolls in its driveway, we took note and set a mission that we couldn't back down from.

So it was late at night and me and a couple of mates set off on an early morning bike mission to this house, approaching it like a military operation. When we got there two people would keep toot (this means look out for passers-by) while the other two dashed over to the car and start pulling at the ornament, yanking it like mad. The thing wouldn't move. It turns out that the Spirit of Ecstasy is attached to the car with a chain going into the grill, so it was one helluva tough job. I yanked it, twisted it, but it just wouldn't pop out. Fearful that someone would soon discover us on the bonnet of this incredibly expensive luxury vehicle, eventually we went for it and just snapped the bastard off the car, tossing it to one of the other lads.

As we all ran back to our bikes to make our speedy getaway, for some strange reason, I went back to the car and carved the words 'TOM WATKINS WOZ 'ERE!' into the side of it. Tom Watkins, if you're interested, was this buck-toothed geeky kid from school, who was a nice enough guy. He was sort of one of our mates, but wasn't part of our group or badge-taxing operation, so why I wrote his name as I did, I have nee idea. Probably so the owners thought it was him, or cos I'm just a right dick!

But it wasn't long before I was to get me comeuppance. The next day, I was at home with Mam, watching a bit of telly, when all of a sudden the front door bell goes. Ding fucking dong!

I didn't really pay much attention to the voices in the

corridor who were speaking to me mam, but here she is to fill you in:

MAM: So the bell goes and I go to answer the door and it's the police. Of course, a million and one terrible things go through me head – every one of them involving Scott! What's he done now, I wondered to meself!

'How can I help you, officer?' I said, trying to play it cool.

'Your son Scott has been involved in vandalising a car!'

I said, 'He's what?'

The officer gave me a knowing wink and said in a louder, more pronounced voice so Scott could hear from where he was hiding, 'We're going to have to take him down to the station.'

When I heard what the policeman had said, I pure shit meself. Did he just say that he was going to take me to the station? Was I being arrested? Well aye! I couldn't go to prison! I just couldn't! I rapidly nashed to me room to tidy away any of the car badges I'd left lying around in case the policeman walked in with a search warrant.

'Scott!' Mam suddenly called out. 'There's someone here to see you.'

Straightening meself up and making sure I wasn't wearing a telltale guilty expression on me face, I joined me mam at the door and said hello to the officer. He proceeded to tell me that he knew that I had been stealing car badges and that I was in big trouble. And, even though I said I had nee idea what he was talking about, the next thing I know me and me mam are sat in the back of his car headed towards the local police station, where I got propa bollocked, had me fingerprints taken and told once again for how bad I'd been.

While the policeman kicked off at me in front of me very disappointed mam I felt like shit. I hated getting told off and felt bad that I had embarrassed meself and, more importantly, me mam.

Me mam would later tell me that the policeman had only taken me to the station to give me a fright, which it did. But sadly, it didn't really scare me off that much (even though he still gave me a caution), as you will see . . .

12

'SCOTT, I HAVE SOMETHING TO TELL YOU...'

'Your dad and I are splitting up!'

I couldn't believe what Mam was saying to me. I knew what the words meant, but I didn't understand why she was saying them. As far as I knew, Mam and Dad were happy together. Sure, they bickered from time to time, but what married couple didn't?

I was lying on the bed in the spare room at Nan and Granddad's when Mam suddenly turned up looking a little distressed. I could tell straight away something was wrong but I never expected to hear those words come out of her mouth.

I started crying straight away. What did this mean? That they didn't like each other any more? Had I done something wrong to make them break up? Was me bad behaviour the reason they couldn't be together any more? Mam wrapped her arms around me and told me these things happen. Sure

I knew *these things* happened, loads of me mates at school had parents who had divorced. But *these things* didn't happen to me. Until now. 'But why?' I pleaded. 'Can't you change your mind? Is there anything I can do to make things better?'

Mam held me a little tighter and told me everything would be fine and I knew then that it was too late.

Obviously now, as a 28-year-old man, I know that if two people aren't happy together, then it's best for them to lead separate lives. But back then when I was 14, I didn't really understand what went into making relationships work. Looking back, I can probably see why things changed between Mam and Dad and I think it all started with the accident.

I must have been around 11 or 12 when Dad had his accident. From what Mam has told me, he'd been driving through town in her red Golf, when a bus pulled out of nowhere and smashed into the back of him. The force of the bang really jolted him, but to start with he felt fine. As a result of the crash, a passenger on the bus started to have an epileptic fit and Dad being Dad – a man with a humungous heart – ran over to help out. What he didn't know at this point was that he had suffered a very serious neck injury and him moving around while he was being a good Samaritan wasn't helping.

I was at school when the crash happened so when I got home later that day he had already been treated for his injuries at the hospital and was sitting in a chair wearing a neck brace. Both Mam and Dad assured me that everything was fine. However, I would later discover that he had been offered keyhole surgery to fix the damaged discs in his neck, but had turned it down cos there was a 50/50 risk that he could end up in a wheelchair.

Things then started to change. His injury meant that he was no longer able to do his job as a commercial diver, which meant that he was housebound for a long time. As a very active man and a top grafter, not being able to work was frustrating for him and that made him unhappy and grumpy and ultimately a nightmare to live with. This is when, Mam told me later, relations between the two of them started to sour.

No doubt hoping to escape the increasingly bad atmosphere at home, Mam took a job with Gill Airways, which meant that she was away from home a lot.

It was annoying Mam not being there, cos Dad and I weren't getting on all the time and I had no one else to turn to except me mates. It was weird not having Mam there, like. I was used to Dad in and out of me life as he worked offshore for so many weeks a month, but Mam had always been there at me beck and call at home. But now the shoe was on the other foot. Only Dad wasn't as easy to live with as Mam. He was strict.

I didn't really understand what went into making relationships work.

Over time, the two of us really began to clash and get on each other's nerves. Everything I did was wrong which I knew anyways, haha. I knew that his angry moods were the result of the pain swell and that he had a lot of frustration at not being able to work – not to mention the ongoing legal action he was taking for loss of earnings. But, selfish as it sounds, that wasn't me fault and I was the kid. I wanted me old dad back, not this strict man with the shorter fuse than before.

But that's the way things continued. When I was really pissed off with Dad, I'd call up Mam at the hotel she was staying at and tell her to come home and she'd tell me she'd be home soon. But I wasn't happy with that – I wanted her there and then.

With no one there to listen to me, I did what I always did and hung out with mates and acted like a right little shit and got up to nee good. As time went on, despite the good times, when we argued a lot it got worse between me and me dad and between Mam and Dad. Mam would still be a softy and stick up for me while Dad tried to make me more grounded. I didn't notice at the time, but now I look back I can really see that there was a change in their relationship.

I really fucking hated the whole situation with them at that point. I never felt as close to me dad as I did before the accident but after it things started to get out of hand. Things are different now though; we've long patched things up and I do love him to bits. This was just back then!

I think when the accident happened his whole life changed. He went from doing things like professional parachuting, climbing in the mountains and causing chaos with his mates to being stuck in the house. And I can imagine that the feeling of having your independence taken away must be devastating. So while I was pissed off with him at the time, now, as an adult, I can totally understand what he went through.

After Mam told me they were splitting up I went to see Dad, hoping he'd tell me everything was all right, or that what Mam had told me was some big unfunny joke. But when I turned up at home, he looked sad and angry and he told me that it was all true, that their marriage was over.

Dad explained to me why he and Mam were splitting and Mam told me her side of the story and cos it's their business I will leave it all there. All I knew was there was no going back and I had to deal with the fact that me life was never going to be the same again.

Life changed pretty swiftly after they announced their split. Mam moved to Ponteland near me nan and granddad, but I stayed with me dad, cos he was staying in the family home where all me stuff was. Of course, I still saw Mam practically every day after school. I kept telling her I wasn't taking sides and that I loved them both equally despite their efforts to chew me ears off, bitching about each other to me. But it was true. Whatever went down between the two of them didn't change a thing about the way I felt about them. They were still me mam and dad, they just happened not to be together any more.

13

MOVING ON

The weeks following the split were tough. Dad was going through a really hard time. Coincidentally, his best mate was going through a marriage breakdown of his own at the same time. Eric had been a hugely successful businessman and owned four Burger King fast-food restaurant franchises. He was a man who had it all. Loads of cash, an amazing house, two loving sons and a happy marriage. Or so he thought.

When his wife announced that she was leaving him, he was devastated and turned to me dad for support. Although they were both going through such a tough, emotional time, I think it was good that they were going through it together as they both had each other's backs and would be at ease when out and about with each other. Sadly, though, I don't think Dad's mate dealt with his break-up as well as me dad did with his, and he ended up turning to booze to ease the pain. Never a good path to take. To watch his best mate fade before his eyes and ultimately pass was so hard on me dad. I was glad Dad had it together and was able to get through each day. But we all miss Eric, he was such a kind-hearted bloke.

Dad was still dealing with the day-to-day pain he suffered in that accident. He was self-medicating at home, smoking marijuana to help him through the pain. He never smoked it in front of me, but I knew he was doing it and of course I didn't mind. In fact – Dad, I hope you're not reading this – I would steal bits of it and take it to show me mates at school and say, 'Look lads, treasure', then instead of showing them the weed just pelt me backpack off some daft cunt's heed.

I felt sorry for Dad; the accident had left him like a shell cos the job that he had loved and spent so many years dedicated to had been cruelly ripped away from him. But fortune was on his side. Not only did he receive a ridiculously massive compensation payout for his injury (I won't say figures, but let's just say that he got enough for him to live the rest of his life without a care), but shortly after Mam had moved out, he dropped the bombshell that he had found love again. Whattttttt?! That was quick, Dad! You've only just broken up and already you've found a replacement for Mam? I thought. I was devastated cos this meant for sure he and Mam were never getting back together. After the initial shock and remembering what Dad had told me about the reasons for the split, I calmed down.

Carol was an old school friend, he told me. In fact, they had actually dated before he had met me Mam. Although they had stayed in touch over the years and Dad knew of her husband who also worked offshore on the rigs it was only

recently that they had got close (er, that saved a question!).
He said to me, 'Look, Carol is like a good friend. I trust her
and I really need someone to be with to help me through
all this.'

Now, most kids going through shit like this would probably have kicked off about these sudden developments, but
cos I knew Dad had been hurt during the split from Mam
I took it calmly and told meself that perhaps Dad needed this
to help him get through this tough time in his life.

As it happens, I got on with Carol like a house on fire. She
was really funny and most importantly she seemed to have
put a smile back on Dad's face. Which was a good thing. Carol
had a son called Jamie who was a couple of years older than
me. When he rocked up to the bungalow to introduce himself
he arrived with two mates in Berghaus Mera Peak jackets –
full-on charvers. But Jamie was sweet! And he said to me, 'So
me mam and your dad are fucking each other!' I creased! He
was a propa radge but had a heart of gold. I was always good
at judging people like this when I first met them.

Carol and Jamie moved into the bungalow shortly after
and everything went smoothly. Obviously Mam was a bit
pissed off that Dad had moved on quickly, but that's what
I expected.

Carol was funny and outspoken and would do anything
for us. She would give me money and help us out with school
work (when I did it) and let me do anything I wanted.

A few weeks after Carol and Jamie moved in, Dad told us
we were moving to a new house in Kenton. I was a bit sad to
be leaving the home I had lived in for so long, but this new

house was going to be way bigger and it felt right that Dad and his new girlfriend should live in a place that was theirs. In me head the bungalow in Kingston Park would always be Mam and Dad's home, the place I turned from boy to man. (I often drive past it now and see if it has changed, have a few flashbacks then fuck off.) Dad's new life was the start of a new chapter for us all and it felt right that we started it in a new place.

I loved having Jamie around and we became really close very fast and hung out all the time. In fact, I used to buzz off seeing him. Jamie really was a propa charver! He was this boy-racer type kid who would get up to all sorts, knocking about on the streets. I could see a lot of meself in him but he was way cooler. He let me hang with him and his mates and we had a lot of fun – by fun yet again I mean getting up to nee good. They scared me a little because his crew were all a bit nuts and they would love to try to intimidate me, but I think they did it all in good fun.

Jamie really took me under his wing and I slowly grew into the man I am today. We'd hang round the streets of Kenton and where he previously lived, together with all his mental pals, being – as you can imagine – neighbourhood destroyers. Like me other pals, Jamie was mental. He was a bad boy, but a bad boy with a heart and he fitted into me life so well cos, like me, he liked to piss about.

I remember this one night Dad and Carol had gone out and left Jamie in charge of me. While we were watching the telly, he turned to me and said he wanted to take his mam's car out for a drive. Of course, I was well up for this and without a second thought we were sat in the front seats of Carol's Corsa propa bombing round the streets of Kenton at full speed. Jamie was a rascal for sure and I loved him for it.

Without fear, he ripped the car down the streets and tore it around corners like he was Lewis Hamilton on glue. As we screeched through town at top speed, I felt both scared and exhilarated at the same time. And I loved every minute of it.

Eventually we reached a long stretch of road. I could feel me heart beating wildly in me chest cos I was just so excited. As we tore down this quiet road I could see the speedometer dial going berserk as we gained more speed and then, without warning, Jamie suddenly grabbed the handbrake and went 'Wewwwww, DRIFTA'. He jarred the handbrake up, sending the car into a fucking time warp, spinning out of control while still moving forward, coming to a rest literally inches from this tree. Looking back, we were lucky we weren't injured or worse. But at the time, it felt like the biggest buzz I had ever felt. Even better than those buckets Benjie and I had had at school!

Jamie really brought the already wild side of me out to its full potential. We used to go on crazy missions together all the time and when he finally did pass his driving test we used to hang out with his mates and go to the most random areas where boy racers would hang out at the coast where people used to go dogging. I was loving life.

As I said, I have Jamie to thank really for making me the MAN and propa cool kid I am today. When he first moved in, he reckoned that while I may have been mad and bad I was still a nerd in his eyes. And looking back, maybe I was.

I remember this one time he took me round to see one of his mates called Steven and when we got to his there were two girls there in his room. Jamie told me to come and join them and say hello, and his mate started waving a condom around and said to me, 'Do you know what one of these is? Do you wanna use it with one of these birds?' And I was like, 'Fucking rites I do!' despite cringing a little bit cos his mate was taking the piss and deffo trying to make me feel awkward, especially in front of these horny girls (who were, by the way, fit as fuck!). What made matters worse, the girls were laughing along with them. I just wanted the floor to open up and swallow me up.

Him and his mates used to meg me all the time. He'd take me out to the park in Wideopen, his old neighbourhood, where all his radge mates hung about, and just leave me at times to go shag some lass. I'd be left with these random lads and lasses who I didn't know height from hair and were much older. They would try to make me feel uncomfortable and take the piss. Some of the lasses were the worst, mind. They used to just come up to me and put me on the spot, grabbing me cock and asking, 'How big is it?', I knew they were only having a laugh but I was shocked at how forward they were. You could tell they were trying to make me feel nervous, but

I just wanted the floor to open up and swallow me up.

luckily Scotty T had been round the block a few times and I think one night I ended up pumping this lass called Trisha in a bush – some blonde nutter who was about three years older than me. Result though!

Although me and me schoolmates had ventured to the Bigg Market for drinks several times before, Jamie was the one who took me into town for the first time. But it didn't end up the way I thought it would.

I was about 15 or 16 and we headed to Bar Beyond, which is up from the Bigg Market in a bar/restaurant complex called The Gate. Although he had found himself a girlfriend, Jamie still liked to go out for a fun night and I think he wanted to pass his knowledge and skills on to his protégé. The bar was heaving, the music was propa pumping, the drinks getting downed and there were fitties everywhere!

Two girls caught me eye and Jamie told me I should try me luck. Not that I needed any encouragement, of course. So I strolled over and started chatting away. It wasn't long before I had the girls eating out of me hand. I was convinced by the end of the night I could probably pull not one but both of these lethal birds. As I carried on with the banter, I was suddenly sent flying into a glass table. As I crashed through it – in what felt like slow motion – I could see everyone turn to stare at us. I was in shock for a minute – I mean what the fuck had happened? Well, it just so happened that the two girls I was talking to were with these other lads and one of them had gotten propa jealous. Cos I was about half his age he decided to lash out and launch me into this table. Next thing I know (it happened so fast that it's all a blur) I was lying in the shattered remnants of the table and Jamie was running over to me and helping me up. It was then I noticed the massive gash on me arm running from me wrist to me elbow and all the blood pouring out of it and seeping into me crisp white shirt. And then the pain hit.

Jamie got me straight out of the club while his mates dealt with the rest (I wouldn't have wanted to be in that bloke's shoes at that point, put it that way). We headed straight home. Creeping in as quietly as I could, I whipped off me shirt and wrapped it around me arm. Jamie came to me room and tried to help clean up the mess but then Dad walked in looking furious and said, 'What the fuck has happened to you?'

I hesitated, wondering whether to tell him the truth or not. I opted for the latter. 'I had an accident, I tripped and fell.' Dad looked at me as if I was mad – he knew I was lying, he always did. But instead of calling me out, he simply took me hospital to make sure me arm was okay. I ended up having it bandaged up for about two weeks, and still to this day have a norty scar all the way down the inside of me left arm!

When Jamie was 17 and had finished school he headed out to Tenerife for the summer, where he worked for some dodgy gangster-type geezer in a poolside bar. I missed him when he was away but sometimes we'd go out and visit him and that was a whole lot of fun. Well, basically the same kind of things we'd do in town back home but just in the sun! Then one day Jamie announced that he had met a girl over there and was staying put. I was gutted, cos I loved having me big bro around back home. But I knew that I'd see him whenever we headed out to Tenerife, which for me and the lads was all the time.

But Dad dropped another huge bombshell on me later that year – he and Carol were planning to follow Jamie and set up home there. Dad said it was to do with his injury that he needed to live in a warm climate so his neck didn't play up as much. He said to me: 'Look, son, once you've finished your GSCEs I'm moving to Tenerife. You can either join me or not.' When I thought to meself, 'Do I fancy going?', I didn't know. That was a decision I was to make later, but in all respect I couldn't leave me mam, me grandparents or me mates behind. So Dad and Carol went to join Jamie in Tenerife and I went to live with me mam in a two-bedroom flat in Darras Hall.

14

Scott Did What?!

I had a bad reputation at Ponteland County High School. But I guess I didn't really help meself. Me, Chad, Lloyd, Benjie and another guy called Ayo made it our business to piss off as many people around us as possible. Well, I say made it our business. We didn't really go out to cause trouble (or did we? I can't decide), trouble just *happened* when we were together.

I remember this one time Chad and I were in the dinner hall sitting together on the norty boy table along with about six others (they stuck us on there for purposefully kicking footballs at the windows to try to smash them) – they thought this would be a punishment. Big mistake. Everyone was on report, which meant we had this piece of paper that we had to get signed after each class to show how well-behaved we had been in the lesson. If you got told off, that would be a mark against you and you could get suspended for a week or two. In some cases you'd get expelled if you kept getting bad marks. I was always on report but luckily I always managed to pass them.

Anyway, while we were chatting shit with each other, the head of the year came over to the table and started having a go at Chad for talking. Another big mistake, cos today Chad was on self-destruct. So instead of replying in a civilised and well-mannered way, he screamed, 'Aaaagggh, AAAAGH fuck off!', then, as the teacher started telling him to calm down, 'Aaaagggh, fuck offffff!', in front of everyone in the dinner hall. He then proceeded to kick over chairs and the table before just walking out of school.

Even in classes, teachers had a low opinion of me. Benjie and I somehow ended up in the same English class and all we would do was mess around. Pissed off, the teacher would move us to the front of the class so she could keep a closer eye on us. But that didn't work. When the teacher turned her back again I would chuck things at Benjie and he'd pelt things back. It was mint! But then the teacher would turn round again and catch us at it, while the whole class sat there watching us like two twats. Of course, I'd be told to stand outside the classroom as a punishment, but even then I'd carry on looking back through the window every so often, still trying to piss off the teacher, making daft remarks and gestures to the rest of the class.

School was a pain. I didn't really wanna be there. I just wanted to go radge or hang out with me mates. At lunchtimes, me, Benjie and the boys (except Michael) would even sneak off to do buckets. The smoke would be so thick (we'd call this a 'propa creamy bucket!') that we couldn't stop

111

coughing and we'd be fucked for a few hours. The first time I tried it, it was fucking class. I could barely see or walk. Just laughed excessively. I wonder now if the teachers could tell when we were on it back in lessons.

While a lot of me mates would knock off class to do this, I actually never did. I'd rather be in class with all me mates and have a frisk. I wonder now if those poor teachers would have preferred it if I had not bothered to come to class at all.

It might sound like I spent all me time messing about, but if you were to read me school reports, I was beginning to show massive signs of improvement as time went on. Although I think that did depend on which class I was in. Cos in particular I liked business studies, geography and the favourite – maths – and I liked the teachers, I was more inclined to work that bit harder for them. For a subject I wasn't so fussed about – e.g., English – I pity the poor teacher who had to deal with me. You know who you are, haha!

But I did have some supporters in the school. Me head of year had loads of time for me, me mam would tell me. He'd say I was really clever when I put me mind to it, and that I was well mannered (see, I wasn't all bad!). Me maths and business teachers said they were very impressed with the work I handed in but that I should really think about paying more attention in class! Hold on a minute, mate, I've got ADHD, remember! (If there's a time to pull that out of the bag, it was a time like that!)

But it was when the school was entered into an annual maths competition that me schoolmates suddenly saw me in a totally different light. Every kid in the UK took part in this particular maths IQ quiz every year. If anyone can remember, there were about 50 questions but you were really tested on how you actually worked out the answers. It started off easy and gradually became expert level, and was an hour or so long, but with me passion for maths, I thought I flew through it pretty easily.

A few weeks later, we were all called into a special awards assembly for our year where our head teacher was to announce how we'd all done, and who was at the top. I expected to do okay, as maths was such a passion for me, but certainly didn't expect to have done brilliantly. The first name the head announced was Michael's, who had the third highest grade and got a bronze. Then he named a couple of other people who achieved the second highest results. Then the head paused with all the drama of an *X Factor*-style finale: 'And,' he teased, 'you'll never guess who got the gold award ...'

There was a dramatic pause as all the kids in the assembly hall looked around at each other trying to work out who the swot might be, as there were a few geeks who sprung to mind. 'Scott Timlin!' the head said. Me face dropped and you should have heard the roar of laugher and disbelief from me schoolmates – it was deafening. I wasn't sure whether to be offended or warmed by the reaction.

After I sat back down and got grief off everyone, the head had another announcement to make ... This was a unique one. It was a Best in School award, because years 9, 10 and 11 had all sat the test. Laughing to himself as he read the name, the head said once again ... 'Scott Timlin!' The whole year was in stitches again, surely someone was having me life!

But I have to admit, I was genuinely stunned by the accolade. I mean, I knew I probably would have done well, but to achieve 99.8 per cent really surprised me. I was so pleased and actually really, genuinely proud of meself – but I styled it out cos nee cool kid wants to look like a swotty nerd.

As I went up on stage to collect me certificate me schoolmates were laughing so hard at me cos I don't think they had ever considered that the super-norty class clown they all knew and loved was actually a bit of a brain box.

Although I was embarrassed by all the attention at school, I couldn't wait to tell Mam and especially Granddad when I got home. They were, unsurprisingly, incredibly happy for me. I could tell Granddad was most proud. In a way I had tried me hardest in the test

I felt that this amazing achievement in some way helped me say sorry.

for him and cos of him. He had put so much faith and confidence in me that I just didn't wanna disappoint him. And in spite of all the trouble and heartache I'd put me family through over the years, I felt that this amazing achievement in some way helped me say sorry for everything I had done and thank them for all the support and love they had offered me.

15

SCOTT FOULS A FOOTBALLER OR TWO

Okay, hands up! I am a norty kid. I can't deny it, or even blame it on me ADHD. I like getting up to mischief. It makes the world go round. I don't think it helped that I had mates like Benjie, Lloyd and Chad who are fucking mentalists, but they were me mates and I loved them. It just so happened that they brought the worst out in me. Thank God we had Michael; he really balanced us out a bit. That's not to say he didn't get stuck into the crazy stuff we got up to, cos he could and still can be just as bad. But he's a lot more reserved than the rest of us. In fact, when I started writing this book I asked him to describe himself and our friendship, and he said this:

MICHAEL: Scott lives in the moment, and lives life large. On the other hand, I'm much mellower and enjoy peace and quiet, so you could say we're opposites in that respect. We bounce off each other quite well, with him reminding me to have fun and enjoy meself, and me calming him down a little as he has a tendency to go off the rails.

Spot on, mate. Spot on! And I love you for it.

But in spite of having our sensible mate Mike with us to provide that all-important balance, that didn't stop me, him and the rest of the boys causing even more chaos in and around the Newcastle area. To be honest, we were like a force of our own. Wherever we went we were sure to leave a mark. Skid mark or otherwise.

So let's get back to the action and present you with Scott and pals' Most Wickedest Mission #564: The Burning Barn.

There was this abandoned barn near some woods where we used to go to drink cider and finger girls. It was a secluded spot so we knew we could get up to all sorts without fear of being walked in on by Officer Pinkie. In the summer it was a nice place to kip rough and sit under the stars. We'd have some of our funniest times there.

Obviously, when night fell, nee matter how warm it had been during the day, an evening chill would nip at us so we would make like fucking girl scouts and start a fire. Now, normally this would happen without incident and we'd wake up the next day to find the smoking remains of last night's fire.

But one time we were all in the barn just snoozing away in front of a fading fire when someone piped up to say the fire needed reviving. Usually we'd just go and find some more wood to throw on the already active fire, but some clever twat decided it would be better to throw some petrol on it (hang on a minute, who the fuck brought petrol with them?).

Anyway, before anyone could stop them from hurling shit loads of petrol on the fire, this fucking tool (hang on, was it me? Me memory is so bad) drenched the place with petrol.

Of course, the fire flared up and spread wherever the petrol had landed. Benjie, who had been sound asleep on the ground near the fire, suddenly sprang to his feet screaming that his foot was burning (his foot was in the fire and his Puma trainer got ruined! They were shit anyway!).

There was nothing we could do to stop the fire spreading. The barn was made of wood for fuck's sake. It was a goner, and all we could do was stand there and watch the barn slowly become a massive fireball and start to collapse as the beams gave way. Then we legged it as fast as we could so we didn't get the blame.

We may have got away with that bit of unintentional arson, but we'd soon be crossing paths with the police again. A while after the barn incident, Benjie and I were mooching around the balcony of the leisure centre next to the high school. From where we were standing we could see the caretakers tinkering around with machinery in their shed. This looked fascinating to young minds like ours and of course we wanted to explore. So when the caretakers disappeared for a bit we jumped off the balcony and wandered into the shed. Now, we had nee intention whatsoever of stealing anything, we just wanted to explore. As we were looking around we noticed that one of the filing cabinets was open and a magazine was sticking out of the drawer. On closer inspection we saw that it was a porno. When we opened the drawer fully, we realised it was jam-packed with pornos! Result.

As we were young, dumb (and full of cum), we stuffed as many of the mags into our coats as we could and ran off to look at them, shoving a few into rabbit holes in a field that we used for cross country at school. But what we hadn't realised at the time was as we were feverishly shoving those slag mags in our coats, we were being caught on CCTV! Shit!

We only realised this when a policeman dropped by school and threatened to take us down the station (oh, me poor mam!). But there is a silver lining to this story. The next time we did a cross-country run and got bored, all we had to do was jump into the bushes, grab a mag and carry on running our merry way holding our porn prize proudly aloft then taking it back to school so we could knock one out in the toilets.

As I've mentioned before, I was a bit of a sporting all-rounder, although I particularly liked those sports that involved throwing – you know, like javelin and discus. Now I look back at it, I think I must have honed those skills on the streets of Newcastle when the lads and I went and got 'chases'. Basically chases were when we'd chuck things at passing cars. Or people. Or anything that moved.

It didn't really matter what we threw – a tin of ravioli, scrunched-up loaves of bread, footballs, snowballs, a rice pudding – as long as it made an impact and pissed someone off we'd be happy. If we made someone run after us – you know, chase us – then that was considered a massive success.

Now we did this a lot. In fact, it was probably the thing we did most of all cos it was it was easy, cheap and fucking hilarious. But as always we did get ourselves into a wee bit of trouble. And on occasions with some rather well-known people.

One afternoon the lads and I were having a kick around in the park near the Sainsburys in Darras Hall – a posh bit of Newcastle where lots of the footballers live. As we were playing, this swanky-looking car purred by. It was obviously an expensive set of wheels, so for that reason alone we reckoned that the rich-boy twat driving it deserved to have his car thunked by our ball. So I sent the ball careering in the direction of the car and BANG! Perfect hit. The ball landed flat on the windscreen and bounced off again.

The car screeched to a halt. We waited for a minute to see if the driver was going to jump out and have a go at us. If he did, and wasn't intent on kicking our asses, Michael would normally play peacemaker and explain that we had simply lost control of the ball and hit his car by accident. But there was nee movement.

Still the car didn't move. I tried to look closer to see what the driver was doing and then all of a sudden I fucking realised. Sitting behind the wheel I could see the furious-looking Newcastle footballer, Alan Shearer. The fact it was a famous person's car didn't bother me so much, it was more that Alan Shearer also just happened to be me dad's girlfriend Carol's nephew. Luckily Alan didn't react, and proceeded to drive off without saying anything to us, but that wasn't the end of it. Later, he got in touch with Carol to tell her that 'her Scott' had bashed his car with a ball and I was made to speak to him on the phone to say sorry! I couldn't even blame Benjie, the bastard had seen me kick the ball!

But Alan wasn't our only Premiership victim. It was a couple of days after New Year and the snow was thick and even. A perfect time to chuck snowballs at each other. Eventually the boys and I tired of thwacking each other in the face with tightly packed snow and decided to start targeting passing vehicles instead. When a swanky sports car appeared along the road, we knew we'd found our perfect victim. We all took a shot and hurled snowballs in the direction of the car, but it was Marcus's weighty ball that made impact, landing heavily on the car's windscreen.

Unlike Alan Shearer, this driver wasn't going to let us get away with it. The driver side door burst open and this athletic blond guy came towards us. He didn't look happy at all and we knew that he wasn't going to come over and pat Marcus on the back for his wicked shot. So what do you do when you see an angry man coming at you? That's right, you fucking leg it. And so we ran as fast as we could along the street. Sadly Marcus wasn't fast enough and this guy caught up with him, launched at him and floored him. Then Benjie jumped on top of him and started digging him until the guy – who we suddenly realised was another famous footballer – ran back to his car.

What a fucking belta! We couldn't believe what had just happened. We had just got into a fight with a Premiership footballer. Those of us who'd scarpered went back to join

Marcus and Benjie who were winded from their rumble in the Arctic. But when we tried to help Marcus back to his feet he screamed out in agony, saying his leg was in pain. I told the boys I thought it best we get home in case the footballer returned, so Marcus and I headed off as fast as we could. I was propa starving and wanted to get back to Marcus's quick. As I power-walked back toward home Marcus told me to slow down cos his leg hurt so much. 'Stop being a fanny,' I shouted at him, looking around to see if the footballer was on the hunt for us.

But it wasn't just celebs we tormented with missiles. We even turned on our own if someone pissed us off (or even just for the sheer laugh). For example, if any of the boys said that they couldn't come out and join us for the night, we'd egg their house. It's just what we did. Or if they had a parent who was a bit of a mardy bastard, that was reason to egg their house too. A mate from school called Frasier, or 'Fraz' we called him, he was one guy who really got it in the neck from us.

He was a lovely kid, who drove a Fiat Punto with a big subwoofer in the back with wires coming out everywhere. He was the only one of us who smoked, he had a wicked chinstrap beard, and his head looked like an 8-ball. He used to join us sometimes when we'd chuck shit at cars driving around Darras Hall. Our favourite vantage point around there was on the roofs of the shops cos if anyone got pissed off with us, all we had to do was jump through the our mate Lloyd's window (he lived in the flat above the shops).

Fraz's dad was always bollocking him for one thing or another and it was clear he didn't like him hanging around with us at all. Can't imagine why, like! You could see that his dad's nagging was pissing him off. But that didn't stop us from taking the mick. Fraz's dad had a habit of leaving him voicemail messages when he didn't come home on time, saying stuff like, 'Fraz, it's your dad here. Get your fucking arse back home now before I put a ban on everything you do.' One of the lads in school got hold of the message and turned it into a dance tune. We all drove around town with it blasting out the window.

Fraz's dad was nuts, like; he was an older bloke with a 'tache and reminded me of Mr Wilson from *Dennis the Menace*. So we used to egg his windows, even when Fraz was in the house. His dad would be furious and come out and tell us to fuck off.

When he went back inside we'd leave and then go back a short time later and egg it again. And then again half an hour later. And then again an hour after that. His dad would go ballistic. Once I remember we did it so much that his dad jumped in his car and started cruising the streets looking for us lot. Fraz even called us to tell us that his dad had gone mental and wanted to chin us. From where we were hiding on the shop roofs, we could see his dad looking everywhere for us. When he pulled over we lobbed even more eggs at his car. This incensed him even more but instead of trying to fight us, he just put his foot down and drove back home where – guess what? – we egged his house one more time.

Me and my mam. I was trouble for her from the very start but she's always stood by me.

I started early. Had me first proper kiss on the island of Tortola with the daughter of a family friend called Alex Kyle. The start of things to come.

Granddad was proper mint. He taught me everything I knew and made me a better person. I still miss him now.

Fuck! Look at me hair! Back then, of course, I thought I looked proper boss.

Flexing me muscles with me mate
Anthony Hutton, who won *Big Brother*
back in 2005.

Jermaine and I ruled the bar
scene of Newcastle. Look at us,
like two Billy Big Bollocks.

Me and the boys on one
of our lads' holidays.
Probably one of the only
pictures you'll ever find
where I don't look pissed
or have a drink in me
hand.

Girls. Boobs. Fit! Wonder
where my hands are!

Me and the boys on holiday. Propa six-pack there, like!

Getting radge on holiday. Mortal!

Eee! It looks like I'm on the bog here. But this is one of my classic green screen one-liner moments which people say they piss themselves at too!

SCOTT

Joining series four of *Geordie Shore* was easy. I just walked in and felt right at home. It helped that I actually knew most of the gang anyway!

Wherever Gaz and I went – even the races – we'd always find the perfect opportunity to scope out some fit bird or two. Helped that we were hung like horses!

I never wanted to settle down with anyone in the show but I came really close with Marnie. She fucked us over a wee bit and when she shagged Gaz I was pissed off!

Me and James with the new *Geordie Shore* lads, Kyle Christie and Aaron Chalmers.

Vicky is a top lass and deserves her success. And long before *Geordie Shore* I tashed on with her.

Always the centre of the party, like.

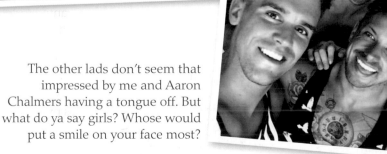

The other lads don't seem that impressed by me and Aaron Chalmers having a tongue off. But what do ya say girls? Whose would put a smile on your face most?

Holly, me and Gaz. We've been through a lot together, but we've come out of it great mates.

Here's me and the *Geordie Shore* crew at the launch of the Birthday Battle series. Look at me grin!

Me, some of my mates, 1D's Niall Horan and John Newman had a blast watching me mate Ellie Goulding in concert. Until one of me mates stripped off in front of everyone.

Hot or what? Kelly Rowland doesn't look bad either! Now she's a proper worldie.

I couldn't wait to get into the Big Brother house, but I never thought I'd do as well as I did.

It was a crazy few weeks in the house but it was fun and I cannae believe I won! What a great night that was.

Darren Day was the main man in that house. Top geezer with loads of stories and he reminded me a lot of me. Daz is a diamond geezer!

Francesca, the girl who's stood by me through the tough times. Who knows what will happen in the future.

Where did it all go wrong?! Screaming girls, booze and money! I'm living the life of Riley!

Me and the boys. I know we'll be mates for life – we have too much dirt on each other!

I wonder where the next five years will take me!

As I write this and look back at the torment we caused that poor man, I do feel bad. We really were a bunch of stupid pricks, weren't we? But we were young and we were having a good time. Of course that's nee excuse, I know, but nee harm was ever meant. I guess we forgot the effect it was having on other people's lives sometimes.

Well, some of you will be pleased to hear that we kind of got our just desserts a while later. Me and the boys were on the Broadway shopping bit of Darras Hall and Benjie was wearing this solid gold chain necklace. These guys pulled up in a car and started talking to us, asking for directions. We were suspicious cos one: we didn't know who the fuck they were, and two: there was something not quite right about them.

Then suddenly one of the guys grabbed the chain from around Benjie's neck, so I instinctively grabbed his arm to stop him. As I did, his mate – the scumbag – pulled a knife out and started waving it in our direction. Without thinking, I grabbed the knife kid instead and threw him on the ground. Then the other kid pulled the chain off Benjie's neck and legged it across the road. I let go of the knife guy who ran with his mate, jumped into the car and sped off. As soon as I realised the lad had twoked the chain, me and a few of the other lads chased after the car trying to hoy bricks at it.

I'm not sure if I was being brave or stupid grabbing a guy who had a knife.

Looking back, I'm not sure if I was being brave or stupid grabbing a guy who had a knife, but I wanted to protect me friend. That's all. I love me mates. We might be a bunch of tossers and twats but we're lovable tossers and twats! There, I said it.

16

DECISIONS, DECISIONS!

So school drove me mad. Although I had a great time with me mates, there was nothing about it that I really enjoyed. It was now 2004 and me and me mates had just sat our GCSEs. Everyone else seemed to know what they wanted to do next, but I couldn't decide. Should I go to sixth form like Michael? Should I go out and find meself a job in the NatWest like Urg (a.k.a. Jason)? Or should I join the Royal Marines like Benjie?

It was all change and I wasn't sure what was going to be right for me. As I didn't really know what career path to take I kind of thought to meself it might be a good idea to go to study A-levels at sixth form. I didn't really wanna, but at least it meant I could coast for another two years to think about what I could actually do as a job.

So I applied for sixth form, which was basically an extension of our high school. But there was a problem. Me past behaviour was proving an issue with the head teacher.

Cos I had been so disobedient over the past few years they wondered whether sixth form was the right place for me.

I obviously laid it on thick and said I was 16, going on 17, and wanted to finally settle down and get serious about me education so that one day I'd get a great job. They seemed to buy it, and eventually agreed to give me a place. But it came with a condition: I could attend sixth form if I kept me nose clean for the first three months. If anything happened in that time, then I'd be out. It sounded like a fair enough deal, so I agreed to it, with every intention of following it through. And for the first couple of weeks, all was good. I was well behaved in classes, I didn't get up to too much mischief and I got work in on time.

And then it happened. I was pissing about in the common room one day with the boys, doing our usual things like rocking the vending machines to try get free drinks out of them, shouting and going on daft. Someone was playing with a ball indoors when it suddenly came towards me. I fucking toe-punted it away and smashed this lass straight in the face on the other side of the room in front of everybody. It was probably another of the funniest things I'd done in me life. We laughed our arses off.

However, the girl who had just been smashed in the face didn't think so. The next thing I know I'm hauled up in front of the head teacher who gave me a patronising lecture about how they had given me a chance and how I had thrown it back in their faces. I pleaded with them that it was just an accident and that I hadn't meant to hit the girl in the face, but I could see that I was fighting a losing battle and I had to deal with the consequences and I agreed to leave. Just like that!

This left me in a pickle. What should I do next? Me best mate Benjie had, as I said, gone off to the Royal Marines. Was that a path I could take? I'd always loved action films and I thought I was a pretty tough guy. Who knows, perhaps I could learn a thing or two while I was training?

I was impressed by the way that Benjie had really turned himself around recently. The two of us had caused so much bother when we were younger that his decision to join the Marines had initially surprised me. It was like all of a sudden he had become this amazingly mature young man (most of the time). And I was glad; he deserved the best.

You see, Benjie had never had an easy life. While I had what you'd call a pretty comfortable upbringing, his was a lot tougher. He lived on the same council estate in Newbiggin Hall that me dad had grown up on, with his mam two older brothers and giant Rottweiler Titan. The estate was a tough place to grow up; gang warfare was rife and houses would be burned down as part of the rival gangs' ongoing battles every other day. Riot police were called to the estate so often they might as well have moved in there permanently.

One of Benjie's brothers was an amazing chef but was also a bit mad and had been in and out of prison most of his life. His other brother joined the army then went on to be in the French Foreign Legion. During our wickedest days, me dad and his mam were worried that we were terrible influences on each other (which I guess we were) and tried to keep us apart (which didn't work). However, over time they both saw that we were incredibly fond of each other and that our friendship ran far deeper than chucking footballs at moving cars.

When Benjie told me he was off to the Marines, I was so proud of him, but I was gutted at the same time that he was leaving Newcastle and, more importantly, leaving me behind. I loved Benjie like a brother and obviously would be worried about his well-being when he was away fighting.

So, after he'd headed off and I'd been kicked out of sixth form, I seriously wondered if the Marines would be a good place for me to progress. I asked Benjie what he thought about it and he shut me down straight away with a very stern 'No way'. I was slightly taken aback by his aggressive reaction. When I asked him why I shouldn't, he said, 'Promise me that you will never join the Marines. If you ever try, I promise you, I will smash your face in!'

I thought it was a strange and extreme reaction to have, haha, but a friend later told me what was behind Benjie's threat (grab a tissue, this is well soppy): 'I just couldn't face me best friend going to war and for me not to be able to look after him,' he'd said. 'I am not saying he would need me to look after him, but the thought of him away fighting somewhere scared the shit out of me. He knew I didn't want him to join, but I didn't really tell him fully how I felt about it.'

Aww, what a lovely thing to say, right? Soppy cunt!

Benjie would go on to serve in Sangin, Helmand province, Afghanistan and complete operational tours in the Gulf of Aden and off the coast of Africa doing counter-piracy work. He was a maritime sniper and did counter-narcotics work in the Caribbean. He would spend almost eight years in the Marines and would go on to enjoy a very fulfilling life, living in and travelling through 50 countries.

He would write or call whenever he could, saying how much he missed me and the lads and how he couldn't wait to get back on the odd weekend to go wild with me. I really missed me partner in crime so much when he was away and I was always so worried about him. But I was proud of him, cos he was doing something important and something he loved.

When he did come home on leave he would splash his hard-earned cash on me and the lads and we'd see how much more he had matured. Even me dad was proud of him and told me he thought he was a changed man.

When Benjie left for Afghanistan, I was devastated. I was so fucking worried for him, I didn't want him to go in case ... in case he never came back. But Benjie said to me, 'Look, you owe me £100 and I will come home again so you can pay me back.' And then he was off.

During his time in Afghanistan, he sent me a few letters and told me that I didn't have to pay him back after all cos when he got home he had big plans to take me and the lads out for a mint night. I really couldn't wait for him to come home to where he belonged. We would have so much to catch up on ...

And then ... we heard the news that shocked us ...

... Benjie was coming home ... FOR GOOD. BUZZING! I was fucking over the moon. He was packing in the Marines and was planning to become – wait for it – a physicist. What the fuck? Benjie a nutty professor? Now he's doing a degree in physics and maths. It's ironic because in school he'd always take the piss out of me for being clever, but his brain was like a sponge, and now he's doing a degree. It's madness.

Years later, when he got home, he didn't go back on his word either. No sooner was he back in the fold than he took me, Michael and Jason out for food, drinks and a night at a casino and told us that he had loved his time in the Marines. 'I was never worried about going to war, I loved it,' he told us. 'It was very intense but that is why I joined. Stories and scars to tell and show me kids one day.'

Right, so where was I? Oh yes, so joining the Marines at 16 or 17 was a no-go, so I decided to sign up for a sport and exercise course at the college in the city centre. That's where I started to meet loads of new people and there were some pretty fit girls there, too, who I banged senseless. It was one of those courses that did exactly what it says on the tin. It was pretty easy and I did it while I considered what me next move might be. I guess the rest of me class had the same idea cos over the next few months, students left the course week after week and eventually it got fucking cancelled.

To make ends meet, I worked part-time in a prescription pricing department for an NHS pharmaceutical company, which was pretty mundane but paid me a good wedge. Of course, I spent it all on going out which meant I was going out – at 17 – every night until three in the morning and bringing girls home to Mam's two-bedroom flat, or to a bus stop, phone box, back alley, even a fucking bush, I didn't give a fuck. Then I'd still be getting up at six in the morning to get the bus in to work where I'd be necking coffees all day and falling asleep on the job.

Even though I was no longer at sixth form I would still hang out with Michael and the guys as usual, and our nights out would end up mental. One evening, me and the gang headed to a bar on the quayside called The Cooperage where we had our sixth form parties (or should I say their sixth form parties) – a really cool 14th-century pub that has sadly since closed down. It was all banter to start, as we necked booze, chatted up lasses and still had people's lives. But suddenly we could hear the sound of shouting and scuffling outside and when we went to investigate we found our mate Marcus surrounded by a bunch of burly lads and it looked like things were going to get nasty fast.

Hoping to defuse the situation (with me fucking fists), I stepped in and tried to break things up. But as I did, some twat punched me in the face. Now, I was only trying to calm things down, but if someone's going to provoke me then I fight back. So I turned on the guy who thwacked me, who then ran off as fast he could and into the back of a cab. But before he could tell the driver to put his foot down, I'd jumped in the back seat with him and started chinning him. No one punches Scotty for nee reason whatsoever and gets away with it, even if I did grab his neck to calm him down. As I continued to punch the fucker, the taxi driver in the front seat kept repeating, 'Get out of me taxi or I call the police,' but I was too busy sorting out this kid's face. The next thing I know Michael and one of the other lads are

131

grabbing me arm and trying to heave me out of the taxi. 'Scott, leave him,' he said. 'The taxi driver's gunna call the police, let's bounce.'

Giving the guy one last smack, I jumped out of the taxi and took a couple of deep breaths. While I'd been busy, everything had kicked off between me boys and the trouble-makers. Fists were flying, voices were raised and some of the guys were caught in headlocks and smacked. As Michael and I headed back to the action, I spied one of the other gang slipping away from the fight without being seen: the one who caused it.

No one punches Scotty for nee reason whatsoever and gets away with it.

'You're going nee where, mate,' I thought to meself, as I watched him try to make his getaway. Without a moment's hesitation, I launched meself at the guy and floored him in a second. But as I did, he dropped this case he was carrying and a bunch of records spilled out onto the ground. Whoops! It turns out this poor geezer wasn't even one of the rival gang after all, but actually the DJ from the bar who was trying desperately to avoid getting caught up in the fracas. 'Oh mate, I'm sorry,' I said to the shaken fella, holding out a hand to help him back onto his feet. As I continued to apologise to this dazed and confused kid, a rapid, beardy old tramp suddenly appeared from nowhere, ran passed us, grabbing the DJ's records as he went by, and took off like a fucking whippet. What a liberty!

Then, like in a scene from a gangster movie, our mate Urg saved the day, screeching up in his tank-sized Vectra and telling our boys to jump in before dashing home.

When the sports course ended I decided that I would try me luck at Newcastle University to study marine engineering and was accepted on the condition I got certain grades. So I was going to need some A-levels after all. I signed up for an intensive course in which I did three days a week studying physics, maths and marketing while going part-time on a Thursday and Friday at the NHS job I had. And I nailed them. Well, I smashed them to start with and then got a bit slack. But when I did me exams I got an A* with high distinctionin physics, an A with distinction in maths and a C in marketing.

Newcastle University was a breeze, though I was so unen-thused about it. I was one of those lazy students who would look out the window and if it was raining, I'd get a bird round for some fanny engineering instead. Or, if I drove into campus and there were no parking spaces, I'd just drive home again. When I actually made it in, I loved the problem solving, the arithmetic and the engineering side of it, but as soon as they asked me to read stuff I lost interest! I would look at the books and think, I won't even get to page one cos I don't have the patience to sit down and read anything.

Instead of moving into halls like most new students do, I decided to move out of Mam's and into this swanky pad on Sefton Avenue, Heaton, that me mate Tom's dad owned and let us rent cheap.

It was the best student house you'd ever seen, except it wasn't really a student house. It was a six-bedroom place, it had a brand new kitchen extension and heated flooring, and there was even a fucking InSinkErator; it basically was a luxury house.

It was mint cos all the boys moving in were close mates. Apart from me and Tom there was Michael, a wacky kid called Karl Jardine, who ran all the fast-food catering in Newcastle for his dad's hugely successful business (he would sit on the couch for so long playing Angry Birds he left an arse print), Gaz Mcgarvey, a nice pirate-looking kid who when pissed was literally the most irritating kid on the planet, and a guy called Jermaine Hudspith, a club promoter who used to knock around as a kid with Benjie and who I had got to know on the club scene and became very close to. But more about Jermaine later.

As we settled into the house, I knew that this was the beginning of a new era in me life, a time of independence and a time of great change! Or maybe just more time to get loose and fucking tear up Newcastle with me knob.

17

'HE'S GOT TWO WEEKS TO LIVE ...'

With Dad and Carol having moved to Tenerife, me finally moving out of home, and not knowing what the hell to do with me life, me post-sixth form days were a very transitional and confusing time. Thank God for Granddad, who would always manage to keep me grounded. With everything that was going on though, I found it hard to see him as regularly as I used to but I'd make the effort to pop round to see him and Nan whenever I could.

Of all the people in me life, Granddad was the one who never let me down. I'd fallen out with mates along the way, I'd bickered with Dad, and me and Mam had had our moments, but Granddad was always so good to me. The only time he ever raised his voice to me was during me parents' split when I took Dad's side in an argument. I'd never seen him do that before and it shocked me. But he later apologised and of course it was swiftly forgotten.

No, Granddad was that one-in-a-million special man who

had me back and really supported me. Without him, I don't know where I'd have been by this point. Probably banged up in the nick!

Impressively for a man of 81, he was still one of the most active people I have ever met. He wasn't one of those OAPs who sit in a chair and watch the world pass by. He was a get-up-and-go kind of guy who could walk for miles without losing breath! Just recently, he had built a conservatory extension in his garden. This man could do anything and I was convinced he was going to live forever.

Only, life had different ideas. Two weeks before Christmas 2006, Mam sat me down to tell me that Granddad had just two weeks to live. 'What?' I cried. 'No!' Tears welled in me eyes. This couldn't be true, me granddad was strong as an ox, how could he be dying? Mam then told me the story . . .

Earlier in the year, Nan and Granddad had been away in the US visiting a cousin who lived out there. When they flew home, Nan called Mam and mentioned in passing, 'Your dad hasn't been well, he has an upset stomach.' Mam, thinking it was just a stomach bug, said, 'Oh, it'll pass,' and thought nothing more of it.

Over the next few weeks, Granddad started work on the extension on the conservatory that Nan had always wanted. Although he had hired workmen to come in to do the hard work, he would occasionally nip off to B&Q to get odds and ends he thought they might need.

Then, at the start of December, Granddad told Nan that he had to go to hospital to have a stent fitted. Nan didn't really understand what the procedure was actually for, but told me

mam she thought it might be to do with his heart, which left
Mam stumped, cos as far as she knew her dad had always
had a pretty healthy ticker. Mam called Granddad to find out
more about what was going on but he assured her what he
was having was just routine.

Granddad was admitted to hospital for his procedure and
then a day or two later Nan received a call from his doctor
asking her to come in to see them. Sensing that something
wasn't quite right, she asked me mam to go with her.

When they arrived, they were greeted by a sombre-faced
doctor who immediately took them into a small private visi-
tor's room. When he asked them to sit down, Mam and Nan
could sense that bad news was on its way. 'I'm afraid, Mrs
Baxter, your husband has pancreatic cancer,' the doctor said
softly, reaching out and taking her hand in his. 'Unfortunately,
with the severity of the cancer, there is very little we can do,
I'm afraid.' He paused to let Nan and Mam take in what he
was saying. 'We think he may have two weeks left.'

Two weeks to live?! Mam and Nan could hardly believe the
words they were hearing coming out of the doctor's mouth.
Sure, Granddad had complained of an upset tummy and he
had been looking a little tired recently, but he was still dress-
ing as smartly as ever, still going for his morning walks. He
didn't look like he was at death's door.

The doctor went on to explain that Granddad had been
diagnosed with cancer several months before and had been
in and out of hospital for regular check ups. It suddenly
dawned on Nan that those regular B&Q trips weren't DIY
errands but actually secret hospital visits.

The doctor also told them that Granddad had not come into hospital to have a stent fitted as he'd told them, but to have a duct to his liver loosened to ease the pain. He also said that Granddad had refused chemo, cos he knew that pancreatic cancer was a strain of the disease that was hard to beat.

Mam and Nan were devastated by what they'd heard. Like me, they thought he was going to live forever.

'I had noticed him looking really tired,' Mam said to me, after she told me the news. 'He was falling asleep all the time. He wasn't as happy in himself. I could tell that there was something wrong, but your nan just said, "Eeeh, he is getting on, you know." But all this time he knew he was ill and he didn't want to tell anyone so none of us got upset!'

'Is there nothing that can be done?' I asked, hoping for a way out, for some miracle cure that no one had thought of yet.

'No,' said Mam. 'It's too late. The cancer has spread and has taken hold of him. It's a cancer that's not very easy to treat.'

Granddad came home a couple of days later and the next few weeks proved to be a tough time for us all. Having been told he had just two weeks to live, we were cautious that he could leave us at any time, so we tried our best to make every day a great one for him just in case it was his last.

And yet, Granddad admirably showed no signs of slowing down. Every day he would get up as usual and carry out his daily ritual of putting on a clean shirt, going to get his paper and he even managed to force down some food in the morning, even though he had lost his appetite.

That Christmas was a bittersweet one cos against the odds he had seen it through, but we also knew that it was most likely his last. It was heartbreaking. While I tried to spend as much time with him as I could, sometimes I found it hard to stay in the room with him cos I didn't want him to see me crying. He had been so strong for me throughout me life and now I had to do the same for him. I wanted him to spend his last few days surrounded by happy faces, not sad ones. He deserved only the best.

For the next few weeks, Granddad's health stabilised and, to an outsider, you'd be hard pressed to tell he was ill at all. In spite of having been given just two weeks to live, Granddad had astonished not just us but his doctors with his strong mental outlook and remarkable resilience.

As April arrived, some four months after he was due to die, I was so excited that it looked like Granddad would be around for me birthday and I made plans for it to be the best one ever.

A week before me birthday, I popped round to help Granddad tidy up the garden. Every so often he'd come out and ask if there was anything he could do and I said, 'Oh no, no, don't worry Granddad, I've got it under control'. He looked at me and said 'I love you', which totally broke me heart. Then he said, 'Oh, it's cold out here,' and went back inside to have a cup of tea. When I finished up I went inside to see him and told him, 'Granddad, I'm away now.' He looked at me, disappointed that I was going and replied, 'Oh, you're going, are you?'

I kissed him and promised I'd see him a couple of days later and went about me business. But it was the last time I ever saw him . . .

That evening, Mam received a call from her brother to tell her that Granddad had taken a turn for the worse and that he had been admitted to a hospice. He passed the next morning.

I found out that Granddad had gone when I popped round to Mam's to find her sobbing on the bed. I threw meself on the bed next to her and held her. When she told me what I had already guessed, me world just fell apart. I knew that Granddad's condition was terminal, but in me heart of hearts I believed that strong old ox was going carry on as he was. When I had last seen him he looked thinner and frailer but he still seemed in good spirits and didn't look like a man who was about to die.

But that was Granddad. He never wanted any of us to worry about him. He never worried about himself, he only thought of what was best for the family. That's why he did loads of things for Nan when he found out about his condition. He wanted her all set up for when he was no longer there so she was wanting for nothing. I admired him for that. It was very brave of him. Living alone in the knowledge that something was wrong must have been so hard for him. He had no one to talk to when he was sad or scared or when he was in pain. Never once did he make us feel sorry him. That's what made me sad. To think that when he was first ill, he lived with it alone.

Granddad's cremation was originally set to take place at St Mary's church on 26 April until Mam remembered it was me birthday. The family decided to change the date and I was asked to be a pallbearer, which I considered an honour.

When the day of the funeral arrived, I just couldn't cope. I had never felt a loss like this before, never lost anyone close to me. What I couldn't get me head round most was that I would never see me granddad again, never hold him in me arms. I was so used to seeing him every week, hearing his voice, watching him smoke his pipe, that I wondered what I would do now. Obviously, time has proved that the pain of losing someone does fade eventually and you are left with brilliant memories of the person you loved. Yes, his death broke our hearts, but he changed all of our lives in some way and he died a happy man, leaving his family with lots of amazing memories.

He had a lot to be proud of. He and me nan had celebrated their diamond anniversary. That's sixty years of marriage. It made me realise that he had had the best life. He and Nan met, fell in love and stayed together for all those years. I wondered if I would ever have what they had, as these days everyone's just fucking each other. Back then it was so easy – get with someone and you're sorted out.

The journey to the church was one of the most painful experiences I have ever endured, driving past the golf club where he had spent his life

I had never felt a loss like this before.

and seeing the flag at half mast. When we pulled up at the church and saw all the many well-wishers, we could see the effect Granddad had had, not just on us, his immediate family, but on the people in the local area who had known him for years. There were so many. Watching the coffin being slid out of the hearse made Granddad's death so real. Resting the coffin on me shoulder, me and the other pallbearers solemnly walked into the church to pay our respects to a man who had meant the world to me, and to say our final goodbyes. I know he's still looking down on me to this day.

18

NIGHT LIFE

So I had left school and left home. I was an independent lad living in a mint house with me mates. I now wanted to make sure that I was making enough money to live off, so I could really hit the Toon hard.

Since leaving school I had worked in that office job at the NHS pharmaceutical company and had found it pretty boring. Then, between me intensive A-level course and uni I did a stint as a labourer and a club promoter. I learnt me hand in a bit of plastering, bricklaying and roofing – don't forget I used to love building Lego kits! – and had already done a bit of handiwork during an extended trip to Tenerife to see Dad and the family. It was hard going and relentless, I have to admit, especially when the weather was hot, but I found it strangely fulfilling and got paid a decent wage for doing it. So what was there to complain about?

I was a young guy launching himself into that exciting independent stage of his life; all I cared about was earning money so that I could go out and have frisk. But eventually I started to think that I needed to find a job that I genuinely enjoyed doing, so I didn't get bored. So I had a think ... What could I do that would keep me entertained? I asked meself. What do I enjoy doing? Well, there was sex. I mean, I loved doing that, but I couldn't think of a way of making money from it that wasn't porn. So that was out ... for now?! Then there was the drinking and going to clubs ... Hmm ... Now there's a thought, like.

Since leaving school, I had hit the bar scene with me college crew and had become very popular around Toon. Cos I have a good manner with people, I soon became great mates with doormen, bar staff and everyone around the city, so I was no stranger to them and they'd welcome me in with open arms every time. Me housemate Jermaine was already handing out flyers and doing PR for bars with a view to becoming a shit-hot club promoter, so he suggested to me that I should try to work in that industry too.

What could I do that would keep me entertained?

One of me first jobs was working on the bar at Blu Bambu, topless! It was one of the most popular clubs in the Bigg Market back in the day. I'd managed to land a job there when I was 17 (but would get sacked soon after because I lied about me age, I'd told them I was 18 and when they found out I wasn't they booted me out! I had a good run though, and when I was old enough to go back I did). Me and me mate

Steven – who I'd met when I started me sports course at college – went and got the job topless hosting there together,
which I absolutely loved; not only cos me body was looking
pretty ripped at the time but cos the girls loved getting their
hands on me! You'd strut through the jam-packed place and
girls would be all over you like a tramp on chips. It was blatant sexual harassment, only I wasn't complaining.

Throughout the night I would often help meself to a
drink – or fucking ten – so I'd frequently end up smashed
and necking on with some of the girls when the managers
weren't looking. Sometimes, some of the more eager girls
would drag me into a corner or outside for a bit more of a
feel-up. But what I found really bizarre is that it was the
older women who had the filthier minds.

I remember one night I was chatting up this group of
ladies in their early thirties who were on a hen night. There
I was, giving it everything, telling them they looked good
(which in fairness they did), cracking a few jokes. Anything
to keep them spending in the bar because I was rinsing them
for tips. As I have the gift of the gab, these ladies weren't
going anywhere. I was making them happy and making sure
they had no intention of moving on. Which they didn't. As
long as I continued to show them attention, they were going
nowhere. And that meant ker-ching for me.

Anyway, as the evening got more and more raucous and
the group got drunker, one of the women sidled up to me
and pressed herself up against me and tried to snog me. That
night the boss was being a propa jobsworth, so I had to give
the woman a Scotty smile and politely pie her off.

In fairness, she looked propa hot for her age, like. Wicked figure, nice face and a belt arse. If I could have I would have given her a swift one in the back room. But tonight it was impossible – the manager was doing me tits in. However, this bird wasn't taking no for an answer. She was well up for a shag and the more insistent she became the hotter I got. So I told her to chill her bean and wait until me shift was over and then I'd catch her up. She seemed happy with that arrangement and we exchanged numbers.

When we met she took me back to the hostel she was staying at with her mates down the road. Still dressed in me Blu Bambu uniform, she led me into her dark dorm where I could see there were about eight sets of bunk beds but couldn't tell if they were occupied.

This bird was rampant and we'd barely got to her bunk before she started hungrily unbuttoning me pants, trying to get me doomstick out. She was wetter than Aqua Man's socks and she knew what she wanted. And Scotty's long cock was here to save the day. I dropped me kegs, pulled off her knickers and lay her on the bed. Cos we were in her dark dorm and unsure of whether or not there was anyone asleep in the room, I tried me hardest to keep the noise down. But when I slipped it in her, she full-on yelped and then as I continued to buck her she groaned and moaned like a foghorn. I tried to cover her mouth so she didn't make too much noise, but it did no good. At this point I didn't even care if there was people asleep as I was well in the moment, then once I'd shot me load I made me goodbyes and left. TE RAAHH!!

It's funny, in me time I've shagged a few older women and they always say to me, 'Oh I'll show you a thing or two.' But you know what? They haven't. I've seen it all before. I'm a belta shag, me – I've often shown them something new and exciting instead.

Bar work itself could be a bit boring. I mean, there were some jobs I did where all I had to do was to hold a sign in the street and try to encourage lads and lasses to go to the bar I was working for that night. Or sometimes, if we were flyering for bars or clubs, like Tiger Tiger and Foundation, we'd get bored, launch the flyers in the bin and go crack on with student birds and stuff. This was the silver lining.

Standing outside shirtless or wearing just a flimsy vest in zero-degree temperatures or heavy rain was not exactly what I called a great night, but the chance it gave me to flirt with some right crackers made up for any downside.

What more could a red-blooded straight guy want than to ogle hundreds of dolled-up girls strutting their stuff down the street. Thank you! There were hundreds of them man, flashing their legs and arses in super-short skirts and jiggling their tits in their tight tops. It felt like I had died and gone to bird heaven. Think of it this way: I was being paid to flirt and neck on with girls as they walked by. Now that's a career path they don't mention at school. If they had, I might have actually sat up and listened more.

For a while, Jermaine and I did loads of topless stints in the local gay bars Powerhouse, Twist and Switch, selling shots. This was a different kettle of fish cos it meant I wasn't too distracted by girls cos there were obviously less of them in the place. But that didn't mean I flirted any less. Oh, I still ramped it up to the max, it was a job after all. But the gay lads were propa sound and were always up for a laugh.

Unsurprisingly, they couldn't get enough of our ripped bodies, even though they knew we were straight. But it's funny, even though you'd expect the lads to be a lot more forward and touchy-feely, I can safely say it's the girls out there who are less shy! In fact, no word of a lie, working in the straight bars and clubs, it's the girls who are full on. I have lost count of the amount of times a girl has stuck a hand on me arse or grabbed me cock, or even pushed me into a toilet cubicle and piped us off. Not that I am complaining AT ALL. But imagine if that was the other way around! In contrast, the gay guys may undress you with their eyes, but they tend to keep a respectful distance. That said, I have never complained about the odd slap on the arse from anyone, boy or girl!

One of our next jobs was topless hosting at Koosday, one of the most popular nights in the city at the time. It was mint. I was drilling girls left, right and centre every night. We'd be glittered up, with the word Koosday written all over our chests and it was just a great time. I was working with one of me best mates and girls as well, getting pissed and feeling mint. I was having the time of me life. And up for anything.

Another job Jermaine and I did together was hosting bar crawls. Basically, all we had to do was to lead a group of revellers from one bar to the next, get them tanked up and move them on. For this job, we didn't have to go topless for a change. Instead, we'd wear colourful T-shirts and a high-vis waistcoat or sash. Of course, while we kept it very professional to start with (for the first ten minutes), by the time we'd reached the second or third bar, we'd be absolutely fucked and forget to tell the group that we were moving on. When the boss found out he'd be pissed off, but we'd blag it and then we'd be back on it another time.

Initially, part of the job would be to sell 'bar crawl' T-shirts to the students which would promote the club nights. Cos Newcastle is such a huge student town, it has a massive drinking culture. It would be a day-to-day thing of us working our magic. It was yet again another mint way of grafting fit birds and getting any amounts of phone numbers. We thought it was gunna be a tough gig trying to convince people to dish out £7 on a pure shit T-shirt with the logo 'skint bar crawl' printed across the front. But our cheeky banter seemed to work a treat and the students were cashing out on T-shirts as if they were made of fucking gold.

So the money started rolling in. This was mint; we were gunna make a fortune at this rate. But then Jermaine burst me bubble and reminded me that for every T-shirt we sold, we were only gunna make a quid.

A fucking quid a pop! Pah! That's radge! I mean, if we sold 50, we'd make just £50 on top of our hourly wage (told you I was wicked at maths!). Not bad, I guess, for a couple of hours' work but as Jermaine pointed out, 'Here, imagine how much we'd make if we made £4 a T-shirt?'

He was right. We'd make loads more. But how could we make more money without raising the price? Surely £7 was as high as you could go with these T-shirts. Then Jermaine had a brainwave that was just genius!

Jermaine dialled the kid who'd employed us and told him that we were having a tough time shifting any of the shirts. As he knew we were usually unreal at selling, he believed us. As time was ticking on, the geezer on the other end of the line said, 'Look, sell the rest for three quid – just get rid of them.'

And so that's what we did. Well, kind of. Cos the T-shirts were selling brilliantly anyways, we carried on charging people £7, sometimes £8, but we were now pocketing £4 quid a top. Clever, eh? In the end I think we made around £200 in a couple of hours. Result.

During this period of bar and club work I hopped from one bar to another, picking up skills all the way. At chain bar Revolution I got some propa bar training where I was taught the ten steps of bar service – such as have a good attitude, the correct way to serve, keeping the bar clean and so on and so forth – which put me in good stead for the future and, indeed, life.

One of me most fulfilling times on the club circuit was working for a place that was run by two brothers called Carlo and Fabio. They were both sound blokes but they were having a problem filling the place up. They had heard that I was like the Pied fucking Piper of the bar scene and asked me to help them turn their fortunes round. I started there with Steven and we tried our best, hiring some young sexy staff to promo the bar, and it worked. People started coming to the bar. We overhauled the till system and explained to the brothers that to get more people to buy drinks you have to buy in bigger stocks of booze and pay for some PR staff. After an admittedly slow start, the brothers soon reaped the benefits of me wise words and saw the bar become a huge success.

The club was called Mist and it was on the seafront in Whitley Bay. Remember? The meeting place of Pancake Face. While this club was a propa class place to work, it was also where I furthered me hobby of fanny, with all the sexy birds working there, and me being boss man, I used to just buck them in the office pretty much every shift. But as I became more and more part of the Newcastle club scene I found meself getting swept up in the lifestyle that went with it. I was already a maniac on the drink, but at least with that I could handle meself. It was also so easy to get caught up in other stuff.

Drugs on the Newcastle scene are so rife these days. Everyone is doing them, literally everyone; they're as much part of the nightlife as booze and just as easy to get hold of. And yes, I admit, I have dabbled occasionally.

I'm not ashamed to admit that for a while I went a bit silly, and was up to all sorts, but at the time I thought it was mint. And when I was raving on MDMA I was on top of the world.

Newcastle is a party town, fact. There's nothing else to do up there except go out and get off your face. I mean, there's literally somewhere to go every single night of the week. There's not just one place that is busy, there'll be seven that are rammed. There are three unis and four colleges, so there are loads of kids out and about looking for a good night.

That's why I did so well on the club nights – there were just so many people out there looking for a good time and I could show them the best bars in Newcastle while rinsing them for money.

But I've seen the bad things that drugs can do and it's not pretty. People have to make their own decisions. Some people let it take over their lives and ruin them, some only take them on special occasions, while others will do it once to see if they like it or not and won't do it again. I've done loads of mad things in me time, some I'm not very proud of, but we all do stupid things and we learn from our mistakes.

19

SCOTTY'S WILD TIMES

Even though I was a fully grown adult, paying taxes and doing me own washing and ironing, I was still a big kid at heart, as were me mates. And when we partied, we partied HARD.

Looking back at those days we were pretty wild and I admit that reading back what we've got up to in black and white makes me feel a wee bit embarrassed, but all I can say is, we were young, horny and totally pissed out of our heads most of the time.

We all have those, 'There was this one night when . . .' stories, those wicked tales that start off with a drink and end up in a police cell.

Well, as you can imagine, I have a million of those stories to share but not enough pages to tell them in. So in the great tradition of those *Geordie Shore Best of . . .* compilation shows, let me give you Scotty T's ten greatest 'There was this one night when . . .' stories.

Now this is definitely the time to flash up one of these:

THIS CHAPTER CONTAINS STRONG LANGUAGE, SEXUAL SCENES AND REFERENCES FROM THE OUTSET AND THROUGHOUT

ENJOY!

1) '. . . I shagged in a baby's cot and vommed on a teddy bear . . .'

Me and me mate 'Sports Course' Steven were out on the town one night and pulled these two girls. When it looked like things were gunna progress further, one of the girls invited us back to her place. She warned Steven that she was a mam of a young child, but that the little 'un was staying over at her mam's that night. Never one to turn down a shag, Steve said he was fine with that and we all went back to her house in Gateshead to get jiggy.

When we got there, the house was like a shoe box, hardly big enough for one person, let alone four hot and horny people eager to shag. While Steve bagsied the bed with his girl, I ended up shagging his girl's mate in the kid's bed. It was about five-foot long and two-foot wide (a tight squeeze), but somehow I managed to do it.

After we finished doing the business, I fell fast asleep in this bed which was pretty much a cot. When I woke the next morning, I was in total agony from having laid in something so small and awkward, with the girl I had shagged pressed on top of me. Me mouth was dry so I reached over for a glass of water that was nearby and necked it in one. Only it wasn't water, it was fucking straight vodka! The result? I literally projectile vomited all over the room and had to use the kid's teddy bears to wipe it up, which I then stashed under the bed before Steven and I took off on the walk of shame home.

2) '. . . we pissed on our sleeping mate . . .'

One night, me, Michael and Jermaine arrived home from a drunken night out. But when we went to unlock the door we discovered it was already wide open. Cautious, we ventured inside expecting either to find someone currently raiding the place or to find the house already robbed. As we walked through the house, everything seemed strangely normal. Laptops were still where they should have been, the TV was still hanging on the wall and it looked like nothing had been moved.

Then Michael whispered that the toilet door was locked. Did we actually have a burglar who had broken into our pad to have a shit? We tried to open the door but it wouldn't budge. Then we called out to see if anyone was inside, but there was no reply. We all looked at each other and then, after a count of three, Jermaine kicked the door in and discovered our other housemate, Gaz, sitting on the toilet – pissed out of his brain, but fast asleep. While we were relieved it was just our unconscious housemate who had locked himself in the toilet, we were still annoyed with him for leaving the house totally open to anyone who was walking by and fancied robbing us. We had a load of expensive gear.

Pissed off with the little twat, we decided to get our revenge on him. First of all by rubbing shaving foam and CIF bathroom cleaner into his mop-like hair, cutting huge chunks out in places he wouldn't notice, then by pissing on him one by one (sorry girls, it's a boy thing). I even managed to do a bent over backwards piss through me legs, which was hilarious. We still laugh at the videos today on Jermaine's phone. That's right Gaz, we still have them all mate! SOZ! As we were planning our next assault, Gaz began to stir, so the three of us hauled him up to his feet and walked him as fast we could to his bedroom, where we dumped him on his bed in his piss-drenched clothes.

The next morning, Gaz came downstairs completely unaware of what had happened the night before. We were all laughing cos he fucking stank. It was a few days later before Gaz finally did find out the truth, when someone saw Jermaine's video diary of the antics on the night and let slip what had happened! Let's just say, he was NOT pleased!

3) '. . . I shagged me mate's shag before he did . . .'

Me and me mate John Paul, who used to always be at our Heaton house staying on the sofas (like a lot of our other pals who wanted to be in the mix with us), were at Liquid nightclub one night when this lethal bird walked straight up to me and whispered in me ear, 'I wanna shag you.' Without a moment's hesitation, being so intoxicated, I replied, 'So do I, you wanna go now?' Ten minutes later we were back at mine shagging.

After I'd left this bird gasping for air, JP texted me to tell me that he was on his way home with two birds from town who are mates and that one of them liked me. I was like, 'Fuck! I need to get rid of this other bird fast!'

Yawning a lot and stretching, I turned to this lass and said, 'Look, me mam is gunna be here at seven o'clock in the morning, I need to get to bed, I think you'd better go.'

Without giving her a chance to reply I started gathering up her clothes, shoes and underwear and guided her towards the front door. Once she was dressed I shoved her outside and pushed her up the garden path telling her I'd like to see her again. Bit of a neck on then . . . goodbye babe! As I'm running back indoors JP rocks up with these two birds. And they are hot.

I flash girl #1 a quick, slightly apologetic smile and dart back inside the house to wash me cock in the sink for round two. The girl me mate had brought back for me was a right little fittie who couldn't wait to get dusted, so while me pal was grafting his bird downstairs, I took mine back to me room, threw her on the still-warm sheets and gave her what she wanted.

An hour or two later, after falling asleep, I woke up desperate for a drink. Making sure I didn't wake the girl in me bed, I popped downstairs to the kitchen where I bumped into me mate's bird. I was like, 'Where's JP?', and she told me JP had gone back into town to pick up his passport (or something) that he had left behind. As we chatted I could tell that she wasn't interested in him. He'd been grafting her but having no luck. So, before you know it, what started out as a midnight chat turned into the two of us shagging on the couch (John Paul's bed).

Next morning, I asked John Paul what had happened with his shag during the night. He said it had been a washout and that he'd just necked on with her. Hmm, interesting, I thought, and I couldn't wait to come clean about what I had done with this lass he got nowhere with, but when he said he had no plans to see her again, I told him: 'Don't worry, mate, I shagged her while you went out.' He looked at me as if he'd just seen a fucking leprechaun. 'Ahhhh man, I was only gone five minutes. How the hell did you manage to get a shag out of her? I was trying for hours.' I replied, 'I'm Scotty T, mate!'

4) '. . . I put a fish up me arse and kicked me pal's door through . . .'

One Christmas, I asked a bunch of mates if I could stay in their spare room for a few weeks while I moved house. With half the housemates going home for the holidays, it left just me and one of me best mates, Brad, in the house.

One night, the two of us went out but ended up losing each other and I'd picked up a couple of girls and brought them both back to the house for a buck. As we stood outside the house I realised I'd lost the fucking key. Me and Brad had promised the other three housemates we'd take great care of it. Too horny to think about where it could be, I spontaneously kicked the door off its hinges to let me and the two girls in. I left the door and proceeded to ride them senseless.

The next day the landlord got in touch to tell Brad how furious he was that the door had been damaged. Brad was confused, as funny thing is I didn't realise he was asleep in the house when I kicked the door through. The owner informed him that the door dated back to Victorian times and was worth a fortune. 'This door has been in our family for 120 years,' the landlord snootily told Brad. 'I want it replaced. NOW' And then he charged him £2,500 for the fucking door, which I had to pay. But how the hell did the landlord know of this incident so soon, when he lived abroad?! It was the next day, for fuck's sake?!

It turned out we had a nosy old lady neighbour, friendly with the landlord, who had been spying on our every move. So when me mate Brad went off home to Darlington for the holidays I stayed on in the house, and one day had a rude awakening. While I was lazing around the living room with some bird, in walked the old woman from next door. It turned out the nosy old bint had a key as she was asked by the landlord to keep an eye on the house.

'Who are you?' she demanded. 'I'm calling the police.'

I was like, 'Fuck. I'm Brad's cousin, I'm looking after the house while he's away, don't call the police!'

But before I knew it, a couple of policemen had walked in, one through the front door and one through the back, catching me in the corridor. Luckily the policemen knew who I was from having been out on the bar scene so I managed to blag me way out of trouble. One of them even agreed with me about this woman being over-the-top and that she shouldn't have been wandering in like that without knocking. Why did she when she knew that everyone in the house was away? The sneaky fucker. I certainly wasn't gunna let the nasty old crone get away with it. She wouldn't even give me a chance.

As revenge, I snuck into her garden one day and took one of her prized fish out of her fountain – this koi carp – pulled down me pants and put it between me arse cheeks head first, after I put out some of me tabs in the water! Don't worry, though, no fish were harmed in this particular revenge attack – in fact, the fish's five-second memory meant it couldn't remember being shoved up me arse at all! LIBERTY!

5) '. . . three fit lasses tried to suck me off . . .'

One night, me and me mates Tino and Adam pulled four girls and brought them back to me place. While Tino was shagging one lass, me mate Adam, who is a stripper and has a massive knob, was generously entertaining two of the girls and I was balls deep in the other one. But, for the first time ever, I was having one or two problems that night. Little Scott just refused to work and I couldn't get it hard. I tried me best, but nothing seemed to work. And worst of all, in its relaxed state, it looked fucking tiny (I'm a grower not a shower, obvs!). I told the lass I was with that I'd be right back.

I went in to the other room and saw two of the girls chilling with me stripper mate Adam (honest, his cock is so big there's enough of it for two people!). Lucky bastard, I thought, but then I realised the two girls didn't look that into what they were doing with Adam and they kept looking over at me with this wanton look in their eyes. Then they got up and walked towards me and said, 'We want Scott!' And I was like, 'Here, are you joking me?' Then the other girl who Tino had shagged came into the room and began to show interest too. They were like flies on shit all of a sudden, getting me pants off as if they were drawing curtains. 'What is going on?' I thought. 'Am I dreaming?' They were looking to get their chops round some meat! But at that particular moment, I didn't have much meat in the tin to offer round. Me dick was that small it was embarrassing, but looking at it they still seemed mesmerised. It didn't make sense as they were pushing Adam off when he was trying to intrude their back doors with his death log. Me mates weren't exactly happy about the fact their girls fancied me more, but tiny dick moment or not, I did finally manage to get me knob back in working order again! Let the damage commence!

6) '. . . I crashed through a table while having a shag . . .'

So, me and Jermaine went back to Adam's for a party at his student house. We didn't really know the lads he lived with. When he passed out drunk, we thought it would be funny to stick spatulas up his arse and mash toothpaste into the side of his head (like I said, we're fellas, that's what we do!).

Anyway, before he'd passed out, he had told us whatever we did at the party, we were not to shag anyone in his mates' rooms. So, a little bit later, I hooked up with a girl, ignored his warning and took her up into this random room. Cos the lock on the door wasn't working, I pushed a wardrobe across the room to secure the door. Only the wardrobe was a crappy flatpack one and collapsed everywhere the minute I moved it. Quickly I gathered up all the bits of wood, hangers and clothes and tried to barricade the door so no one would walk in after I finally got to shag this girl.

Looking around, I saw that the only place in the room that wasn't now damaged was a desk. 'Should I shag this girl on the desk?' I thought to meself. Why not! So me and the lass start necking on and I slowly worked her across the room and slammed her out across the desk. As we started to get passionate, we suddenly heard the creak and crack of wood and all of a sudden the table collapsed beneath us and we crashed to the floor, cutting all me leg open. The random room was fucked. It was left with broken pieces of shite Ikea furniture and dirty student clobber everywhere but at least man's got his tackle wet. Me and Jermaine left after this. Adam was not happy the next day when he called me. 'Scott! What the hell did you do to me mate's room?!' I fully denied it all, like. I told him that we'd left once me and Jermaine finished Colgate-ing his whole head. Haha.

7) '. . . I pissed in a washing machine . . .'

Me and some mates went to a bird's party in Jesmond one night. When we got there it was already pretty crazy and everyone was propa pissed. One guy was lying on the floor while other guests were shoving a condom-covered fork up his arse. Ouch! As the evening progressed, I started getting with this girl who also lived at the house. But by the time we started necking on, she was totally wrecked and out of it.

So I left her lying on the couch and noticed that there was washing in the washing machine. I was so pissed that I thought it was a good idea to dump a load of oats and Marmite into the drawer where the powder goes, also adding Cheerios and tuna. Then I pissed in it and set it on a cotton hot wash. Then, in another moment of fucking madness, I grabbed an iron, plugged it in and started ironing the floor, burning massive lines into it. The poor girl who lived there was so absolutely wrecked that she didn't know what the hell was going on. Never heard anything back about that, though I don't think there were that many people at the party she wouldn't have been able to pin the blame on me. If you're reading this Sophie, 'twas ME!!

One guy was lying on the floor while other guests were shoving a condom-covered fork up his arse.

8) '. . . me mate threw a TV out of a window . . .'
Michael, Benjie and I were out in Tiger Tiger one night and I started tashing on with this nice Scottish lass who worked there. One thing led to another and she asked me back to her student halls. Cos I was with me mates, Michael and Benjie,

I asked her if they could come back with us. She said yes as long as they didn't wake up her housemates. While me and the girl got it on in her room, Benjie, who was pissed as hell, suddenly kicked off, tossed a chair across the room, stamped on a Playstation, ripped the TV off the wall and went to launch it out of the window. Luckily I came out of the bedroom at this point and managed to catch the TV by the power cable, with the TV dangling out of the window.

By coincidence, two security men were passing below and started yelling up at us to find out what was going on. To calm things down, I leaned out the window and told them that me mate was sleepwalking and did this kind of thing all the time (while DVDs were flying over me head). Luckily the security men bought the story and went on their merry way! 'What a clown!' The girl was pretty pissed off and she asked us to leave. Just before we left me mate walked into some random room where a kid was asleep. He threw a chair and shouted, 'Good morning, Vietnam!!', while flipping this kid's bed upright with him still in it. The kid, who looked like a pile of mush against the wall, got the shock of his life. I was dying with laughter. Benjie lost it on occasions and when he did he just went on a rampage. Hilarious!

9) '. . . I was arrested for knocking out a rugby player . . .'

I was enjoying a night at Liquid (lesson learned: don't go to Liquid!) with some mates when this big burly rugby dude came bounding over and tried to start with me. I'm not even entirely sure what it was about, but he was really aggressive and then started pushing me. Cos I started pushing back, all his rugger mates suddenly surrounded me and tried to intimidate me. Rugby Guy kept on and on at me and then went to hit me. Sick of his constant stirring for a fight I decided to end it there and then and took him clean out in one dig to the face.

To start with I was worried I had killed him, as for a moment he didn't move. Even his mates started after that and I banged one of them straight, too. The rest were taken aback by what had happened and inched backwards slightly in case I wanted to give them a killer right hook, too. Luckily, Rugby Guy started to stir, so I was relieved I wouldn't be up on a murder charge. The police were called by the bar security and I was hauled down to the police station where they questioned me. It was looking likely I was gunna get charged for assault, but then the police checked the CCTV footage and could see that the rugby dude and his mates were the ones who had provoked the trouble and went at me first.

10) '. . . I fixed me own broken nose . . .'

Me and some mates were having a fun night at Liquid (yes, that place again, you'd think I'd learn a lesson, right?). A massive fight kicked off. I'd been minding me own business but then tried to break it up. Some divvy obviously thought I was involved and headbutted me in the face. Before I got the chance to hit him back or find out what the fuck he was doing, he took off, leaving me with what looked like a broken nose.

Me and the lads went straight to the hospital to get me nose sorted out but cos I was left to wait so long to be seen, I twisted me nose back into place and went home. Hard, aren't I?!

I hope you enjoyed those stories. Please don't try them at home. Or at anyone else's for that matter. I know, I know, I'm a massive idiot, and I've done some right radge things when I've been pissed. See, I told you that what you see on *Geordie Shore* is just the tip of the iceberg!

20

GIRL WOES AND BOY CODES

I love women, me, I really do; I enjoy being with them and having sex with them. Like I said before, I loved what me nan and granddad had – that long-lasting relationship where they found love and stuck with each other for the rest of their lives. I think that is amazing and I really do one day hope I find that special person. Who knows? Maybe I already have.

But when I moved out of me mam's and started living away, I was rampant. I was like the fucking Duracell Bunny. If I saw a girl I'd probably shag her as soon as I saw her. But, just like at school, I get easily distracted.

And yet over the years there have been girls who have come into me life and meant something to me. Who have been more to me than just a shag, way more!

A lot of the girls I have fallen for I have met when I've been out in the bars, mainly as one-night stands which have developed into happy relationships. Sadly, so far they've not lasted as long as I'd have hoped, either through me own fault (necking off with someone else when I've been out) or cos me lifestyle has never been one that most girls find easy to deal with.

I guess in some ways, me lifestyle pre-*Geordie Shore* was just as bad as it is now. When I was working the bars and the clubs, me job was essentially to flirt and seduce girls into me bars. It was just what I had to do. Also the job was a pretty full on one, cos it wasn't a nine-to-five job; I had to work evenings, a time when most couples snuggle up on the sofa, watch Netflix and chill. While me girlfriend would be at home, I'd be in a skin-tight vest telling strangers how fit they were and, depending on how pissed I was, I might even be sticking me tongue up their fannies in the VIP areas.

But there was one girl who I was madly in love with who kind of played me at me own game.

I was at a party with me mate Steven from the sports course and saw this totally stunning girl across the room. She was small, had long dark hair and the most gorgeous face I had ever seen. I knew there and then I had to go over and speak to her. So I bounded over to her as I did, and started grafting.

There was one girl who I was madly in love with who kind of played me at me own game.

She was a funny lass and a good crack who had me hooked straight away. She also said she had an ex-boyfriend who was still in the picture, which didn't faze me at all cos the more time she spent with me the easier it would be for her to forget him.

And so we started dating (i.e. fucking and talking a lot). I was working in the bars at the time so I wasn't able to give her all the attention/penis she wanted and I think that pissed her off sometimes. But I would explain I had to work these hours cos I needed to earn money to live and to make sure she was happy.

By this time I'd decided that I wasn't as into me education as I thought. It wasn't for me. The bar and club scene I was now immersed in was so much more exciting and offered me more about life than uni ever could. I wanted to progress through the promotions industry like Jermaine was doing. Jermaine had become a massive inspiration to me. He started handing out flyers and hosting like me but then took control of his own shot girls and started up a small business providing shot girls to all the bars and clubs around the city. He was doing so well. He had begun to create what would later expand into the impressive empire that he has today.

Me girlfriend said she understood the situation and that she was happy to live with the way things were, but when it didn't suit her she would make it quite clear that she was pissed off.

Don't get me wrong, for the most part we were happy. We were together for about 18 months so it lasted a good while. But there were times when I would suspect that she was seeing her ex-boyfriend and that would destroy me. The idea that she was seeing someone who had at one time been special to her broke me up. I would try to keep it to meself but then sometimes in the heat of the moment I would let rip and confront her about it. She would cry and deny it, but the rumours I kept hearing were from reliable sources. People would tell me that she and her ex were seen together or that his car had been parked in her driveway. These stories came from different people; surely they couldn't all be wrong or telling lies?

Me mate Karl, who lived with me at the Heaton student house, used to date her best friend, who was crackers. We used to double-date a lot, but his girlfriend would never let him out of her sight. She was attached to him at all times and always asked where he was or where he was going. He didn't mind her doing that, that's what most of his girlfriends did. I was hoping that I wasn't being like that with me bird. I wanted to give her her freedom, but then I didn't wanna be taken for a fucking fool.

As time went on and I heard more and more rumours about me girlfriend sneaking around – which she would continue to strenuously deny – I became less interested in the relationship and got to the point where I got with other people when I was out working, busting birds left and right. They were sly kisses, quickies against a wall, but I sensed that the interest that I had had at the beginning had faded cos I no longer trusted the dick.

As I said, there have been times too when I have truly fucked things up quite easily by meself. I was dating this stunning girl called Holly. She was, of course, gorgeous and came from a pretty rich family. I can't for the life of me remember how we met but we were seeing each other for a while. She was very good to me and she bought me things all the time like an iPad and a TV. Yeah, she was a keeper.

Except I was a dick and chucked it all away by getting with a girl called Katy who lived two or three doors down from us on Sefton Avenue, Heaton, but who I had actually met on Facebook. What Katy and I had was just a bit of fun, nothing special. I just used to go round hers and blast her now and then. It was never meant to be anything else, and of course, Holly was never meant to find out. But stupidly Katy and I conducted most of our flirtatious banter on Facebook, which I used me iPad for.

I guess you can see what's coming now. Yes, one night Holly came over to see me. After a bit of fooling around, I drifted off to sleep on the bed. While I snoozed beside her, Holly noticed me Facebook page was open on me iPad and skimmed through some of the messages, as any nosy and insecure girlfriend would. Sadly this nosy and insecure girlfriend had every reason to be suspicious cos it didn't take her long to stumble across a damning conversation that took place between me and Katy, that ran along the lines of, 'Yes, it was amazing when we met up and shagged.' (Lesson learned: always log out of Facebook when the bird is in the room.) So they weren't even messages that could be misconstrued as anything other than 'I shagged you!', haha!

Punching me in the head to wake me up, Holly demanded to know what the messages meant. (Er, pretty obvious, no?) But before I could get a word out she started screaming at me about how hurt she was by what I had done and then stormed out. To be honest, I couldn't blame her. She had caught me with me pants down, so to speak. It was me fault and I only had meself to blame. But I really liked her and

171

certainly had no intention of hurting her. I left it a while before I embarked on me peace mission, and thanks to me talent of wriggling out of trouble I managed to convince her that it had all been a big confusion and that someone else in the house had been flirting with Katy using me account as a joke. Unbelievably, she seemed to lap it up, bless her, and we carried on dipping and dating for a few more weeks before we finished for good.

On the subject of relationships, the ones that I have found strongest in me life are those with me mates. And I'm not just talking about the Michaels, Benjies and Jermaines in me life. We fellas tend to look out for each other and make a deal from the outset that we will never shit on each other's doorsteps.

A lot is said about lad codes and we all abide by them and agree to never go behind a lad's back. These are the two most important:

RULE 1: You never go for a girl that your mate is seeing/ engaged to, nor do you go with your mate's propa exes (previous girlfriends), unless you're in love, but then you would discuss it with him first. It's just not worth the arguments and falling out.

RULE 2: If you're just getting into a girl (which is just meeting, on and off shagging, or the odd cinema date) and it just so happens your mate likes the same girl, then you say to the other, do you mind if I went there? And if they're just getting into them then that's normally okay.

The only time I have ever got with a girl who has been involved with a mate is when I have met a girl who I didn't know was a pal's bird and cracked on with her. If I find out there is an involvement with a mate, then I will stop it straight away. You see, I'm very loyal to me mates. Me pal's girlfriend could stay in me bed and I wouldn't touch her. It wouldn't even cross me mind. I know it sounds weird cos I am a bit of a sex pest and I love fanny, but I won't look at me mates' girlfriends like that, even if they are beautiful. I don't even have a slight attraction, so the temptation's never there.

Oh, but if a girl cracks on to me and she has a boyfriend, that's a whole different rule. I've got with a girl who has been attached and the boyfriend has come for me and I said to the lad, 'What your girlfriend does has nothing to do to me. You need to speak to her.' That's the girl's fault! She forgot to mention she had a lad!

21

LADS' HOLIDAY COMPILATION

The lads' holiday. Sun, sea, sex and fucking wild escapades. Stick a bunch of guys together and you can expect sheer bedlam. You've seen the *Inbetweeners* movie – they're just like that, except we're not a bunch of socially awkward gimps! And of course, with me and me mates involved, we always manage to take it one step further. Here's a compilation of some of our best!

Tenerife

From about the age of 16, me and the boys went on a holiday every year, mainly to Tenerife, where me dad, Carol and Jamie lived. It was ideal to go there cos they were always able to sort us out with a cheap place to stay and would look after us if we ever needed anything.

The holidays usually followed a formula: countless missions during the day, pool hopping or cliff jumping, then

174

a couple of hours to get ready with drinks before we hit the strip that night and partied, bucked and digged a couple of pricks trying to ruin our night. But each trip would offer up a different story to tell the folks back home.

Normally we'd head out to Veronicas – a shopping centre that had been turned into a place jam-packed with bars selling cheap booze. First up we'd head to Yates's and the Mett bar where we'd line up a bunch of fish bowls to start our night with a bang! Another bar in particular had a miniature golf course and served a 50-litre fish bowl in a bucket! We would get absolutely fucked and smash up the cactus plants with the golf clubs. One time we were there we started driving golf balls over the bar into the strip and into the apartments nearby. Fucking lunatics, like. Of course, at a holiday destination like this you are gunna be spoilt for choice for bars. What we would always look out for were bars that had good drinks deals, played quality music and had the prettiest girls, then we would spend the rest of the night trying to get the girls pissed.

Of course, most nights would end up with us all mortal and one of us waking up in a bush or face down naked on the floor of our hotel room, as me mate Michael did during one of our trips to Tenerife.

We'd all been out on the strip for several hours when Michael suddenly announced that he'd had enough and was heading back to the hotel. Benjie and I told him we wanted to hang around the strip a little bit longer cos we already had a couple of sexy Scousers in our sights. Once we conquered our targets it was pretty easy to convince them to come back to ours to party some more, but when we got back to the hotel, we realised we didn't have a key to get in.

We started knocking on the door but there was no answer, then looking through the window we could see Michael lying on the floor totally naked. Worried that he might be ill or worse (dead), we tried knocking again but still there was no movement from Michael. In a bit of a panic, Benjie used his Marine super strength to rip the window out of its slot so we could climb through. Once we'd climbed inside and leaned in close, we realised that Michael was in fact breathing but was just dead pissed and totally out of it! Benjie and I looked at each other and we both said at the same time, 'SHAVE HIS ARSE' and fell into fits of laughter. Once we'd collected the tools for the job – shaving foam, razor – one of the Scouse girls piped up and offered to do the dirty deed before they got taken to the master bedroom for a seeing to.

In case you're wondering why Michael had ended up naked on the floor, he reckons – cos of course he can't actually remember – that he got home, had a shower and had to lie on his makeshift bed of two sofa cushions on the tiled floor (there were six of us in a two-bedroom and Michael had pulled the short straw) and fallen asleep.

A couple of nights later, our mate Fraz – remember him? The guy whose house we used to egg – had brought a girl back to the room but of course, us fellas couldn't let him simply just buck her. Nee way, we had to make sure that we put him off his stride as much as we could. While he was pumping away in his room, I dashed poolside and brought back one of the massive parasols, burst into the bedroom and started ramming this giant umbrella at his arse while he was mid-thrust in this bird. Neither Fraz nor his lady friend were very amused.

On another night during this particular Tenerife trip, we took part in a crazy drinking game in an Icelandic bar where you had to drink the shots in the fastest time. Unsurprisingly, with our expertise in the art of drinking, our team – mainly thanks to Urg and his speedy shot downing – was the overall winner. However, the multitude of shots didn't sit well with Jason and within seconds of receiving our winning T-shirts and bottles of wine he was puking over the balcony. A lot, into some fucking fish pond at the bar. The fish were having a field day going berserk bopping in and out the water scranning his chunder. The owner was going mad because Urg wouldn't stop, and eventually barred us from going back.

We didn't wanna carry our prizes around the strip with us all night, so before the next bar we stashed them in a bush nearby. But when we went back to get them, they'd been stolen.

Of the four or five trips we did to Tenerife, the funniest one was in 2010, the year of the Icelandic volcano eruption that grounded planes across Europe. Now, we'd already booked our tickets way in advance so you can imagine our disappointment when we heard the news that every plane in the UK was banned from taking off. I was adamant that I was still going cos I had been looking forward to this trip and some fucking volcano wasn't gunna stop me from getting there.

The boys – this time round, Tom, Jason, Michael, Benjie, me – agreed and so we booked some train tickets to take us down to London so we could get the Eurostar to Paris. When we got there we were told the only tickets available were business class ones for the next morning. It would be an extra expense of £900, but that was no problem cos WE JUST WANTED TO GET TO TENERIFE as soon as possible.

So we booked ourselves into a hostel for the night so we had a base to dump our shit and then hit the local sights of London's Leicester Square. While Michael sloped off to a casino with Urg, Tom, Benjie and I went to Yates's to see what kind of girls we could find in these desperate times. Of course, we found two lasses from Russia who we brought back to our hostel and banged. Fuck knows where Benjie went, probably for a swim in the Thames.

Next morning we got the Eurostar to Paris and on arrival Michael suggested we eat something at this posh-looking restaurant across the road from the station. He ordered something called a steak tartare, which in his mind sounded like a well-cooked bit of steak. Sadly the reality was not as appealing as he had hoped for – raw minced meat. And the worst part was, the nasty dish could have paid for an entire night out for the same price.

Still intent on getting to Tenerife, we inquired about whether we could catch a flight from Paris to Tenerife, but even this far south, the planes had been affected by this fucking volcano.

So next we tried to hire a car, only we were apparently too young to hire one (you have to be 25). Luckily, I spotted a girl at one of the counters who looked like she knew fuck all about what she was doing, laid on the charm really thick and managed to get her to sort us out a car.

So Michael and I took turns driving the 1,200km journey from Paris to Madrid. I had to get used to the other side of the road first, as on departure from the Enterprise Rental place I drove the wrong way up the underground car park to get out, coming face to face with a fucking police car at the top. Luckily the policeman noticed we were tourists, made me reverse the whole way back down and fucked off. Lucky bastards! Lazy bastards Tom, Benjie and Jason slept in the back seat the whole way while we drove. It took almost ten hours to get there but we were just pleased that we were getting closer and closer to our destination and the land of fanny.

When we went to dutifully return the car to the Madrid office of the hire company, they pulled us up on our age and told us we should never have been issued with a car in the first place. We couldn't be fucked with the hassle after that monster journey and just snapped.

'Well, what do you want us to do, you prick? We're here now!'

Now we'd arrived in Madrid, we just had one more journey to take before we could immerse ourselves in the sun, sea and sex we were hoping to find in Tenerife. But we would have to wait until the next day before there was an available flight to take us to our holiday paradise. So of course we did what we always did during stop-overs – enjoyed the local delights and got pissed. And poor Michael got so pissed that he spent part of his night wandering the streets banging on hotel doors looking for a place to sleep as he couldn't hack the airport floor. How he didn't end up in a police cell or a hospital bed is anyone's guess.

And then finally we arrived in Tenerife. Only thing is, the flight took us to the north of the island and we wanted the south, so the final break of the travel bank was a €150 taxi ride to the south. We could have kissed the tarmac, we were so happy. Cos we had spent so much extra cash on the journey, we decided to extend our trip slightly so we could enjoy our stay that little bit better. That trip, like previous adventures, was a riot. We were staying slap bang in the middle of town in the top-floor apartment above Yates's bar on the strip, which meant we could look out and scope some fitties before we even hit the streets! The rest of the trip was the usual recipe of sun, sea, sex and boozing – I shagged a lass over a wall in the kids' playground next to our hotel who howled like a wolf – but this time round we also managed to break some laws.

On one of our very few non-drink-fuelled days out, we decided to do something cultural and hired moon buggies to go and visit the massive volcano in Mount Teide. When we arrived at the site, which was mightily impressive when you saw it up close, we found a break in the perimeter fence of the national park and ended up having a drag race in the volcano crater. Before we knew it, the authorities turned up blaring their fucking sirens and started chasing after us. When they caught up with us they tried taking our passports off us because it was a national park and the areas we

were doing doughnuts on were sacred land or something.
As usual, we managed to talk our way out of too much
trouble.

Cos there wasn't much going on back home at that time
(it was between finishing sports college and uni) I decided to
stay out in Tenerife for the rest of the summer. Dad was over
the moon that I was hanging around and lined me up with
some labouring work on a building site, which earned me a
pretty good wage. While I was there, I hung out with me
brother Jamie, who was now settled on the island hosting
nights and DJing, and hit the strip smashing girls, left, right
and centre.

I also caught up with Lucy, who I mentioned was a singer
from Manchester that I'd met on a previous trip. She was a
lovely girl and really clicked with the boys. She was kind of
like a 'holiday girlfriend', so whenever I was over in Tenerife,
I would always hook up with her if she were free.

Actually, come to think of it, I had another holiday girlfriend based in Tenerife called Jordan. She was a stunner and
I would also see her whenever I was over. Of course, I was
careful that neither girl would ever cross paths – not that
either relationship was serious, but you know what girls are
like. They get possessive, as I found out to me cost one night
when Jordan caught me snogging some girl and kicked off
big time. I dunno why she went mental cos we both knew
where we stood, but she did and it pissed me off. I would
later find out that she tried to get her own back on me by
attempting to stick the lips on Benjie, who (abiding by the lad
code, page 172) pulled away! Now that's a mate!

Magaluf

Now, as much fun as our Tenerife jaunts were, our 2009 trip to Magaluf was absolutely mint! I was a bit short of money at the time so decided to fly out for the second week to catch up with Michael, Karl, Jermaine, Adam, John Paul and Urg. When I arrived at the hotel Fiesta Tropicana, Jermaine told me not to bother checking in and come straight to the room, which I did.

As soon as I dropped me bags, Karl took me out to the pool where we necked a few well-earned drinks and then – cos we were a couple of dicks – we started chucking limes up at some of the hotel room windows. What are we like, eh? We carried on doing this until some massive black lads started shouting at us and then gave chase. Karl and I legged it back to the room, slammed the door shut and fell on the beds laughing our tits off.

All of sudden, those lads started banging on the door and burst in. At that point, Karl and I stopped laughing and we jumped up to square up to them. But to be honest there were five of them and they were built like fucking brick shithouses.

As we were about to change our tack and be all nicey nicey, the rest of our mates, Michael, John Paul and Urg, who'd been in the next door room enjoying a sambuca tea party, appeared behind them and that luckily managed to calm the irate guys down. Actually, in the end they turned out to be pretty cool.

What a way to arrive in Magaluf – with a punch-up. Well done Scott, you tit.

Magaluf – a.k.a. 'shag-a-scruff' – really was a belta and it was crammed full of daft events. One night Karl and I went and pulled a load of palm tree branches off the trees and turned our hotel corridor into a jungle. It took a lot of effort for the two of us to make the corridor look as good as it did, but strangely the hotel staff weren't particularly keen on the stunning new look.

While we were there I had a fair bit of fanny action, but one particular sexual liaison ended up disastrously. I had picked up this girl and brought her back to our room. Cos me mates were on the beds, I took the girl into the ensuite bathroom and shagged her in the bath in the dark. When we were done, I took a step to get out of the bath, slipped over, whacked me head on the sink and totally knocked meself out. I only woke up a while later, stark bollock naked, with me mates standing over me trying to revive me and this poor sweet girl looking on and asking if I was all right.

Later in the week, we made like tourists and hired pedaloes and splish-splashed in the sea. Then we spent the afternoon cliff jumping, which was absolutely exhilarating. Back home in Newcastle, we used to spend a lot of our free time doing back flips off a bridge down by the river. But this was different. Standing on the cliff edge and looking out across the sunlit ocean and breathing in the warm air made us feel like we were in a paradise (but the reality is that it was fucking Magaluf). And when we leapt off the edge and plunged toward the crashing waves below, it was times like these that made me the happiest kid ever, so if you haven't been on a propa lads' holiday, get it sorted. They really are something special.

As the fellas and I sauntered back to our hotel, a gorgeous girl came bounding up to us with a big friendly smile on her face. She was fit as a fuck and I was all ready to jam me face between her bum cheeks when she said to us, 'Hey boys, me name is Pascale. How do you fancy appearing in a Basshunter video tomorrow?'

Back in 2009, Basshunter – or Jonas Altberg as he's known to his pals – was the dog's bollocks. He was a Swedish dance producer who had had massive hits in the UK with songs like 'Now You're Gone'. He was a bit of a legend, but his songs were real floor-fillers. Although the songs were big hits in their own right, Jonas created more of a buzz about them by telling a soap opera story over the course of several videos which followed the ups and downs of his 'relationship' with a gorgeous girl, played by a fit Iranian-Norwegian ex-porn star, model Aylar Lie. Each video ended with a shock cliff-hanger. And this one, for a song called 'Every Morning', would be no different.

'Fucking rites,' we said. Pascale – who would later date Mario Falcone briefly on *TOWIE* – was thrilled and gave us all a big hug. 'Come on, let me take you to meet the director.' So we followed Pascale to Oceans Beach Club where we chatted for a while with the director. He seemed nice and he appeared to like us and told us that he'd be in touch.

Thinking nothing would come of it, we hit the strip and kicked off another night of fun and debauchery. While we were drinking at Mambo's, Pascale called to tell us that we had the gig and that Jonas was really excited to have us join him in the video and explained where and when we had to meet them the next day. That was just the news we wanted. What a mint experience this was gunna be.

We met the crew next morning by one of the big hotels by the beach. There were loads of people involved in the video, lots of techy types, a couple of models, one of whom was Pascale, and, of course, the stars of the video, Jonas and Aylar. Fuck me! I had always thought Aylar had looked stunning in the videos, but up close and in the flesh, she looked PINGING! Jonas came over to us. He was huge, really good-looking and really nice. 'Lovely to meet you boys, I am so glad you can come and do this with us. It will be a lot of fun!'

One of the production people came over and told us what was gunna happen. The shoot would last all day and would take place in three locations, here at the hotel, another scene on a yacht and a night shoot down on the beach. It sounded ace. The story for this video had Jonas planning to propose to Aylar, but every time he whipped out the ring to do the deed one of his mates would tackle him to the floor. Michael had been chosen as one of his 'friends' – you can see him at the start of the video walking along the promenade just behind Jonas. Jermaine was asked to be the cheeky pal who kept stopping Jonas from proposing. The rest of us would be his close mates hanging out with him on the yacht.

The first set of shots was done at the hotel and it was fun watching Michael get his actor face on. It was interesting to see how a video is actually made and it was a lot different to how I expected it to be. They play back the song so Jonas can lip synch along to it and shoot the same shot two or three times and then again from a different angle.

In the afternoon, the whole crew moved down to the marina to hop on the yacht for the next scene. This was our scene and the vibe was like a classy booze cruise, with the emphasis on classy. More extras were involved in this section, and there were some right fit bikini-clad birds joining. I didn't know where to look. I was walking about with a crowbar in me shorts.

Sadly we didn't have much of a chance to do any sharking cos the boys and I were required to do our close-ups, if you please. The director told us that we had to sit around Jonas as he sang to camera looking cool and sexy. Easy! It's a natural look for me!

They shot and reshot the scene several times. Then they moved onto one of Jonas's attempts to propose. Now it was Jermaine's time to shine. When the director called action, Jonas started chatting with gorgeous Aylar and then reached into his pocket to pull out an engagement ring. Cue Jermaine, who suddenly appeared from nowhere and tackled him to the floor. Again, like the other scenes, this one had to be shot several times but it never got boring cos this was such a bizarre experience for us and we were lapping it up.

Then we shot some cut away shots of us partying on the boat, which gave us a chance to chat up the other extras that had been scouted for the shoot.

As the sun started setting, it was time to head back into shore for the final scene. This was set at a beach party and once again Jermaine would be centre stage as he tried to stop Jonas from popping the question. Not only that, in this scene, he was required to make out with one of the gorgeous extras, the lucky bastard!

The shoot ended with the finale of the video, where three extras come running up to Jonas to tell him that Aylar has been swept to sea. Oh God! What a cliffhanger, eh? (If you wanna see if Aylar survives, check out Basshunter's follow-up video for 'I Promised Myself'.)

Cancun

While nothing could compare to starring in a music video, me trip to Cancun a few years later was sensational for totally different reasons.

Me and some mates, including Brad and Michael, had jetted out to Cancun in Mexico for Spring Break, a time of the year when young, hot, fit American school kids full let loose. Weirdly, we were there at the same time that the cast of *Geordie Shore* were filming for the series before I started in it.

We were staying in this fantastic hotel called the Parnassus, where we became pally with some blokes from London. There was only one reason for this holiday – birds, birds, birds. Every day we had beach parties at a place called the Oasis, an all-inclusive resort that you can't book through an English travel agent, as it's an American Spring Break hotel. It was insane, lush hotel and the amount of up-for-it party girls grinding away in string bikinis was fucking mindboggling. It was like I had died and woken up in fanny heaven.

Of course, as we spent the day there, we met a couple of girls who took a shine to us and told us that we could come and join them later on that evening at the hotel. Cos security was strict at their hotel, they had sneaked us in by pulling us up over the wall and into their room. But security had seen us so we dashed down the corridor to find somewhere to hide. Cos we were causing a bit of commotion some girls poked their heads out of their room and one bunch of girls told us to come and join them. And boy, it was like a scene from a porno.

No sooner had the door closed than three girls fell to their knees and started sucking me off, while me pal is shagging one on the balcony. This was like some kind of crazy fantasy and nothing like the days when I used to get me thrills from blasting a charver girl by a bus stop in the freezing cold.

It was like I had died and woken up in fanny heaven.

As the girls continued to play me like a didgeridoo, security started banging on the door. Shit, bad timing, as I was just about to. . . .

'Oi,' I called out to me mate, 'we need to get out of here.' I ran out to join him just as the girls opened the door. Me and me pal hopped over the balcony. We had moved so fast that me mate didn't actually get a chance to put his shorts back on and had to run back to our hotel starkers.

Our hotel also had rules. No one was allowed back into a room unless they were wearing a wristband. So, in order to get girls up to our room, we told the concierge that we had lost our band in the sea and asked if they would give us another one. When they did, we'd snap the band and take it out with us with a bit of Sellotape stuck to it, so when we got a bird we could Sellotape the hand to her arm. It was fucking mad carrying Sellotape out every night! But it worked.

I'm not exaggerating here, but the girls in Cancun were so up for a buck! It must have been the heat! And these girls were not shy! In fact, many of them were up for beach sex. But you had to be careful if you were in the mood for an al fresco frisk. Not just cos sand gets all over your cock and fanny, but cos sex outside is not allowed and you could get into a lot of trouble. Which made the sex even more exciting.

I loved Cancun so much that I returned the following year. Sometimes people say never try to relive a great time, but fuck that! Cancun the second time was just as brilliant as the first time round. This time I returned with me mate Will who came on the first trip and one of the lads from London we'd met the previous year.

This time we managed to stay at the propa party hotel, the Oasis Cancun, and it was mental. All we ended up doing was taking girls back to the room during the day to shag them, one, two, three . . .

I remember there was a fit bird I wanted to shag but me pals were getting ready in our room and her mate was sleeping in hers. So we started running around the hotel, looking for somewhere to shag. We knew we couldn't do it in the toilets cos there were security cameras and people everywhere.

So then we found one of the hotel restaurants that hadn't opened yet. So I started shagging her behind a table but cos

I was so horny as I had been waiting so long to shag her, I put it in and came straight away. To spare me embarrassment, I tried to distract her from the situation and said, 'Shhh, I think I can hear someone coming. We can't do it here; we're gunna have to leave it here.' The poor lass had no idea I had already shot me load.

The second trip to Cancun really was amazing for girls. It was also where I lost me foursome virginity. That's right: me+girl+girl+girl. What a legend I am. This foursome actually happened by complete fluke, and still to this day I can't work out how I ended up in such a pickle. But from what I remember it started off as a normal night out with the boys. Apparently I went to get a taxi back to the hotel cos I was smashed, and as I got in a cab three girls jumped in. Next thing I know I'm at their hotel and the staff are demanding I hand over me passport and phone in exchange for being allowed in their room, making a big scene. I eventually agreed. Next thing I know I've got one girl sitting on me face, the other taking me for a ride and the third – I have this vague memory of her naked trying to get me Nike blazer trainers off for about half an hour (anyone who has had these trainers will know what I'm talking about when I say they're a nightmare to take off in a hurry). That night I think I got violated, to be honest, but I wasn't complaining. I got me end away WITH THREE GIRLS. Adding to the already over-the-moon feeling I had in the morning, seeing the jealous looks of staff while they gave me belongings back and watched three girls help me to me taxi (before they each gave me a snog) made me feel like a king! All hail SCOTT 3 COCKS!

Ibiza Part 1

And then there was Ibiza ... Michael, Benjie, Urg and I went for a week. Again, this was a lad's holiday we would never forget, mainly cos I think we spent around five grand while we were away, not to mention it nearly killed us off!

Our stay in Ibiza coincided with the Ibiza Rocks festival. We had already booked two deluxe rooms, but when we had arrived, one of them had a leak, so the hotel put us up in another room, a penthouse, where they normally put the bands performing at Ibiza Rocks. So it was pretty cool and we couldn't believe our luck. The room was fucking lush. The balcony alone was the size of a tennis court, and just everything about it smacked of luxury. A couple of days into our stay there we were told our original room had been repaired but we asked if we could stay where we were instead. And they said yes! Fucking get in!

During your stay at the hotel, each room has a credit card assigned to it with about £400-worth of money to buy drinks. So Michael and Urg had one between them and so did Benjie and me. Of course, you know what we us rascals are like. Benjie and I nicked Michael and Urg's cards and used them both up in one day. For the first four days of our trip, we didn't go to one club cos we were literally too fucked, tanked to the brim with alcohol and spaced out from all the treats we'd encountered. The island is fucking mental. I'm sure the police don't even care. Our first propa experience sent us Jacob's Cream crackers! We didn't sleep for four days and we were in a terrible state. I can't remember a thing. It was as if I'd been in a coma and woken up with me wallet nicked, cos over there in a flash your money is gone!

Compared to me normal success with getting me dick wet, Ibiza didn't really have the same vibe as Magaluf and Cancun. All the girls seemed more interested in getting wrecked than actually cracking on or having any banter. But Scotty T still managed to bag a few, of course!

There was one night we invited all these girls up to our room, and we had this massive fight with blue paint. I dunno what happened but we just went mad. After nesting a girl in a bath of blue paint, I started doing loads of mental shit: I ran at the wall, jumped up in the air and crashed through a table. We smashed clocks, chairs, anything we could get our hands on, even throwing them over the balcony. We were fucking lunatics. And then cos we had blue paint all over us we had to change into other clothes so we could go out and party. For some reason Benjie ended up wearing just a tutu with nothing underneath, walking around the West End with his manhood out for everyone to see. People were that fucked I think they were talking to his cock.

This was the holiday where our mate Urg had a bit of a crisis of confidence. Now, he is one big fuck-off guy, with a rugby build and he is dead good-looking, but his problem is that he's really self-conscious. We were out one night and me and Benjie were chatting up a couple of girls. Jason came back from the bar and started talking to a lass who I'd been talking to and I'd necked on with. We took the girls back to the hotel and it all kicked off between Jason and that girl about something. I came out to calm things down and he

said to me, 'But she's mine,' and the girl looks at him horri-
fied and was like, 'But I don't like you, you're really creepy,
and I've been getting with Scott.' And he said to me: 'But
I pulled her, I saw her first.' And I was like, 'Look Jason,
I actually got with her before you walked over. You just
didn't see. She doesn't like you, she's not gunna get with
you.' And he said: 'I never pull girls, this always happens,
cos I have seven chins and you've got one.' I was like, 'What
the fuck you on about, mate?' hahaha!

See, zero self-confidence. It's annoying cos that's how he
loses birds. He can pull anyone he wants, but he ruins it and
says it's the way he looks, and we say, 'No, mate, your looks
are helping you, you clown egg!'

Anyways he calmed down, time went forward and I ended
up dusting that lass, but we were that tired after trying to
calm Urg down I think I fell asleep on the kid!

On the last night we went to Deadmau5 at Amnesia
and poor Jason was vomiting everywhere. And he carried
on being sick from 2 a.m. and all through the morning and
all through the flight back home. Ibiza just wasn't for him –
poor Urg!

22

STALKED BY MTV

So *Geordie Shore* had kicked off back in 2011 and had made quite an impact on the nation. Mainly a negative one. While fans of the show couldn't get enough of Gaz, Charlotte, Holly and the crew getting mortal and bucking people in the shag pad, certain elements of the press poured scorn on the show and said it was 'filthy' and suggested that it 'showcased human life at its lowest'! But that's miserable old bastards for you. Yeah, the show was explicit and unlike anything people had seen on TV.

Compared to *TOWIE*, which at its worst saw the Essex dwellers 'mugging' each other off at Sugar Hut bathed in a glossy shimmery glow, *Geordie Shore* unashamedly showed young Newcastle, the party scene, as it was. There was sex (loads of it), girls crawling on their hands and knees smashed out of their faces (right, Charlotte?), girls pissing in their beds (aye, Charlotte, is that you again?), lads scrapping and even more bucking. It wasn't exactly the kind of show you'd want your nan to see, but you could understand why young people couldn't get enough of it. And the proof was in the pudding when ratings for the show gave MTV its all-time biggest figures. Working around the club scene before *Geordie Shore* aired, I'd heard the rumours that MTV were visiting bars and clubs in the city (me city!) looking for real Newcastle lads and lasses to appear in a Geordie version of their reality show *Jersey Shore*. A few of me mates had already been approached, like Gaz Beadle, James Tindale and Vicky Pattison, and someone told me that me name had been suggested to them a shit load of times as a potential candidate cos I was very popular on the town scene and was an absolute nutter. I was chuffed that me name was getting mentioned, but to be on a telly show? NAR! It just wasn't me. I was just mad Scotty T who liked going radge, drinking and shagging. Little did I know that those MTV scouts wouldn't stop pursuing me until they found me and I finally said yes.

So I had watched a couple of the episodes at the start cos I knew Gaz, James and Vicky from being divvies around town with us lot. We didn't really knock with them loads, but knew each other well enough to say hi and all that.

I was also really curious to check out what the show was actually like, as MTV had been sniffing round me to join it. And it seems that they were still trying hard to track me down because I was always on the move.

Eventually I was in a bar called Spy Bar on Osborne Road, the main street in Jesmond, with a few of the lads and I was approached by a fit lass and some other kid with a camera. They stopped me and asked if I had a minute to speak.

I said, 'Why have you got a clipboard?'

'I'm Lauren and I'm from MTV. We're looking for people for *Geordie Shore*. What's your name then?'

After a few minutes of winding them up I told them.

'Me name's Scott,' I said and their faces propa lit up.

'Ah, so you're Scott, we've heard a lot about you!'

So I said, 'What have you heard, like?'

'A lot of people have been telling us that you'd be amazing for the show.'

'Have they now?' I asked. 'That's wicked, but I don't think I'm interested to be honest. It's just not for me, like.'

After they chewed me ear off for half an hour I gave in and gave them me number anyway. They kept messaging me to go to their office for an interview for the show, but I still didn't really fancy it so I kept sacking it off. I wasn't that fussed about being on TV and I wasn't sure if it was gunna be worth me while. So then Lauren and her camera guy came to Dirtiz, a weekly club event that Jermaine and I had started, and asked if I would say something to camera for them.

Thinking it would get them off me back once and for all, I went outside and answered a few questions on camera, like, who are you, how old are you, what do you like doing, to which I said, 'I like pulling girls and shagging them!' They seemed happy with what I gave them and then they went on their merry way. Thinking that was the end of it, I carried on focusing on Dirtiz – or at least grafting birds.

A few days later I got another message telling me their big bosses had said that me interview was the most natural video they'd seen, and they thought that it was hilarious.

I was happy that they liked me and that but I still couldn't be arsed. I didn't wanna be on TV. Besides, I was currently seeing a lass and didn't think starring on a show like *Geordie Shore* would work right now, so I said, 'Nee joy, I'm not interested!'.

I had met this other lass called Ashleigh Defty about a year and a half before, through some mates. She was stunning – long dark hair, gorgeous face, fit body. A typical Scotty T-worthy girl. She was very special to me and we fell deeply in love very quickly. Our relationship was so strong that I didn't bother with anyone else while I was seeing her. Which says something. I literally saw her every day. We had such a laugh and never wanted to be apart.

But, over time, as the club nights became more and more frequent and I kind of lost meself in that world (still trying to find meself now), our relationship altered and we became a little bit distant from each other. I still loved her, of course, and I still stayed loyal to her but work began to consume me to the max.

It was around this time that MTV were after me. Ashleigh and I were facing difficulties, and Gaz (pirate-looking lad), Michael and Jason (Urg) had suggested that we get ourselves to Australia on a working holiday visa. It didn't take me long to decide what to do as various factors in me life were suggesting I try something new anyway. I had done two years of me degree and needed a year out.

The lease on the house that I was living in was up, which meant it was a good time to reconsider things. I had also reached the conclusion that as much as I loved running the club nights with Jermaine, I didn't have the passion and commitment to doing it as well as he did and so I told him that I would be going away for a while. I was also feeling totally lost in a world of non-stop partying and all that went with it and felt like I needed time to clear me head and take stock of me life before I did a series of really stupid things. So without hesitation I told Michael and Jason, 'Count me in, boys.'

They were thrilled, but when I told Ashleigh me plans, the reaction wasn't so great. She nearly took me heed clean off me shoulders!

She was foaming and I think she thought I was abandoning her. But she knew it was good for me to go as we weren't on the best of terms by this point. The last few weeks I had been going wild all the time, partying, drinking and all sorts. And I rarely went out with her to the bars cos it would end up in an argument and I wouldn't be able to flirt with other girls without her kicking off. Not that I was doing anything bad. I just like to flirt and be meself and I felt that I couldn't. I was such a wild kid and we would argue a lot about daft things. I think she wanted more from me but I just couldn't give it to her. But we agreed to stick together and that we'd pick things up when I got back from Oz.

With the lease up on the house, I went to stay with another mate from high school called Alex at his dad's banging mansion in Darras Hall. At about 24,000 square feet, it was the biggest house in the north-east and boasted a cinema, gym, club, pool and spa. I stayed there for about two or three months and it was amazing. Alex and his family were so good to me and let me bring people over to the house all the time, like.

One time, while Alex's parents were away, we had a few people over for a party and I was shagging someone in the jacuzzi and I jizzed in it. The next week Alex told me that he was with his dad by the pool and he was tasting the water, and saying to Alex, 'Hmmm, the pH level of the pool is off. It tastes a bit funny.' Alex, creasing himself, was like, 'Aye, Dad, I dunno what's up with it, like', while remembering that I had spunked all over the thing the week before. NIGHTMARE.

With help from me nan, who had just recently won a fair whack on the lottery, I was able to buy meself a car, and me ticket to Australia with some spending money, too. I was really looking forward to getting away from Newcastle and the shit I was getting meself into and I couldn't wait to just be with me best mates again. What with Michael getting a girlfriend and Benjie having been away a lot with the Marines, I was looking forward to some quality time with me boys.

After a god-awful 24-hour flight to Brisbane we checked ourselves in at this propa stinking hostel. I was like, 'Here, fuck this, let's go and find somewhere decent.' For the first few days, we spent loads of money cos the drinks were that expensive over there. I spent a fortune. Then, on the third day we were there, we hired this daft hippy camper van with a tent on the roof that folds out and we drove to various cities up the east coast trying to find work. It was great fun driving along those big roads and we had such a laugh together! It was but like old times, just with less shagging (gutted!).

After stopping in many cities on the way we eventually got to a place called Mission Beach in Queensland and checked into Scotty's Beach Hostel. In spite of its name, Mission Beach wasn't a Spring Break type place like Cancun. It actually catered more for families but it had a cool and relaxed atmosphere and there were a lot of young backpackers coming and going.

We spent hours just hanging around and drinking goons of wine (a goon is like a box of wine with a built-in pourer – they got you smashed). We didn't get pissed often, though I did get to shag a lass on the couch in the TV room, smashing her while *Family Guy* was on the telly. WINNING! It was a nice change of pace. It felt like we were all grown up. The people at the hostel said they would be able to sort some work out for us on a banana farm.

Then, just a day before we due to set off to the banana farm, the folks from *Geordie Shore* got in touch again. This time the big head honcho from MTV, Steve Regan, wanted me to Skype him for five minutes. Which I did. What I didn't know until later was that I had positioned the camera at the wrong angle so all Steve could see was half me head. I'd just got out of the shower as well, and was in me boxers. Ha! He asked me various things like, 'When did you last fall out with a friend?', 'How did it get resolved?', 'When did you last cry?', 'What made you cry?', 'Who is the most important person in your life?' In the end, Steve said they really wanted me for the show and that I was the only potential housemate they hadn't seen in person. If I agreed then I would go home then head straight into the house.

When I said goodbye to Steve, I sat back and thought to meself, 'What the fuck should I do?' This wasn't going away. They had spent months chasing after me, begging me to screen test and be on the show, and I kept throwing it back in their face. And yet they still wanted me (I would later hear that the more and more I said I didn't wanna see them, the more they wanted me to do it! See, playing hard to get does work!)

I sat Michael, Jason and Gaz down and asked them what I should do. They gave it to me straight and told me it was a fucking mint opportunity and that I'd be a mug not to give it a go and that I didn't have to stick to it if I didn't like it. What they said made sense, like. I had reached a turning point in me life and yet I didn't really have a plan. This *Geordie Shore* thing might not have been something I had set out to do, but people obviously thought it was something I should try. So I told meself, yes, I'm gunna do it. But before I confirmed everything with Steve and the MTV crew, there was just one person I needed to run it past – me mam! But I'll let her tell you about that conversation:

MAM: Well, he calls me up and of course, I think the worst. 'What's up?' I said. 'What do you need? How much?'

'MTV have been on the phone,' he says. 'You know that programme *Geordie Shore*?'

And I went, 'Yeah.'

He says, 'Well, they want me to do the show and I dunno what to do.'

And I said, 'Did they want you to come home?'

'Yes,' he said.

And so I asked, 'Are they going to pay for your air fare?'

'Yes,' he said.

And I said, 'What if they don't want you? Are they gunna pay your airfare back to Australia?'

'Yes,' he said.

So I said, 'Do it!'

And he says, 'Right, sound.'

23

GEORDIE SHORE

The journey home from Australia gave me a lot of time to think about things, about life, about the future and about how fucking fit one of the stewardesses looked in her tight-arse uniform strolling up and down the aisles (I get so horny on planes).

I was excited about what was coming up and joining the show, but I wasn't sure what to expect. I mean, I'd never really chased after this opportunity; it had just landed in me lap. So in some ways I knew that whatever the outcome of it I wouldn't be disappointed.

I understood that there were some people in this world whose lifelong dream is to be part of a show like this and all the shit that comes with it. But it was never on me radar. I was just happy to be doing what I was doing.

Being famous was not something I craved at all. I just wanted to have a laugh. And that's what life on *Geordie Shore* was gunna be – a laugh. I mean, at the end of the day, I was gunna be paid to do what I do in real life – drink and shag. So what more could I ask for?

When I landed, I went straight home to Mam's, where MTV had a film crew waiting for me. The rest of the cast were moving into the house the following day so I was told they had to get this footage of me preparing to go into the house ASAP.

Having a camera crew there didn't faze me. In fact, I genuinely didn't notice it as I shoved me clothes into a bag and bid farewell to me mam and mates (one of them chased me as I left with his pants down – Adam, the tit. Ha!) as requested. I guess that's why I come across well on camera, cos it felt natural.

Cos I would be living in the *Geordie Shore* house for five weeks without much access to me real life, I spent me final night with pals and me mam. Me mates were buzzing for us and reckoned I was gunna have the time of me life, while me mam was a bit more cautious about me decision cos she had seen a few episodes and had been slightly shocked by the banter. By the girls mainly! But she said to me that she trusted me to do the right thing and made me promise I wouldn't show her up on the telly.

The next morning I was up bright and early (which never happens), ready to be taken to the house. I wasn't nervous, cos I had nothing to be nervous about. I knew most of the people in the house already, so it wasn't like I was walking into a fucking chess club. I related to these people. But then I was wary that for the next five weeks I'd be without me mobile phone and I wouldn't be able to message fanny on

Facebook or see me best mates every five minutes like I was used to. That was gunna be the toughest part.

Before I'd signed up to the show I had asked the production team what was in store for me and I have to admit what they told me sounded pretty good. We'd be expected to stay in the house for five weeks, with a three-day break in the middle. We'd get paid for our time in the house to make up for any loss of earnings as a result of being cooped up.

As we were under the care of the production company, we wouldn't have to spend a penny on anything – everything like food, drinks, bills would come out of the production budget. The same with nights out. Whichever bar, club or location we would go to on the show, all of it would be organised and paid for by the production team beforehand. If we fancied something from the shop we wouldn't have to lift a finger, except to point, as we'd have a house runner to go out and get whatever we wanted. So that'll be ten packs of condoms ... actually no, wait, sack them off, just get me some fags please and a Mars ice cream!

When I finally pulled up outside the *Geordie Shore* house in Wallsend, I suddenly became excited as I knew it was finally time for the Scotty lift-off. I wanted to make a big impression and not just fade into the house. Wearing the same pink T-shirt and jeans combo as the previous day (as requested by production for continuity purposes) and me hair looking slick as fuck, I thought I was looking lethal.

'Alreet!' I said, as I burst through the door, full of smiles and sheer swagger. I could see that Gaz and Vicky were pleased to see me and Gaz fucking shat himself when he noticed we were both wearing the same bright pink tee. Great minds, eh?!

Holly, Sophie and Charlotte smiled back at me, but I sensed they thought I was gunna come into the house and bow down at the altar of Gaz! As if! I'd have an altar of me own!

Ricci, Charlotte and Holly were the only ones of the cast that I'd not met before but they seemed sound. And it was great to see the others and meet them properly for the first time.

Gaz and I had mutual friends and knew each other well from the party scene. I'd knocked about with him a few times and we were mates, but just hadn't known each other long enough to be propa close. We never had a real cuddly friendship. I knew James to say hello to cos he was mates with Jermaine, so I knew he was a good lad.

Once I was in and made me introductions, I felt at home straight away and all me apprehensions about joining the show disappeared. It looked like this was gunna be a fucking frisk. And I was determined to make the most of me time there.

I wasn't the only new castmate this series; there was also a guy called Dan Thomas-Tuck. He wasn't as cocksure as me but he was a sound kid. Unfortunately for him he got himself slaughtered on the first night and came on too strong with Charlotte, who at this point had a boyfriend in the real world. This pissed off Gaz who had to straighten him up and give him some ground rules. Everyone thought he came in trying to be like Gaz but he just didn't have what it took, poor Dan. He made me laugh though and made me time in there. I kind of wish he was still in the show, actually, cos he took a lot of shit but took the banter well.

After Gaz and the gang showed us around the house, it was time to relax and make ourselves feel at home. Once the drinks were getting seen off inhibitions were lowered and that meant I was horny. When I had walked in I was feeling cocky as hell and had clocked Holly straight away. She was a new face and a new pair of tits to me and I fancied her and wanted to bang her. At some point in the evening I got me knob out. She grabbed it and sucked it. The next thing I know I'm blasting her in the bathroom. I wouldn't say she was me type, I just looked at her and thought, 'She's worth a gan.'

From that night on, Holly liked us – when you're stuck in the house like that it just happens, especially for the girls. The thing is I liked her, but it was never going be a big Gaz-and-Charlotte type relationship.

A few of me mates asked me when they saw the episode if I thought I had encouraged Holly into thinking that something more would come after we shagged. But I didn't think I had. There was no meaning behind it, it was just a bang. I just wanted to get me end away. I think with me willy! It runs off instinct. It's like a pneumatic drill.

From the outset I had no plan of what I was gunna do or how I was gunna act. Why would I plan? It was reality TV so I just went with the flow. Everyone knew I was a character. What they see is what they get! I am always like the way I am. I'd managed to impress the people at MTV by just being me, so they let me run free.

Gaz and I got on like a house on fire straight away, like I always knew we would. We were both pretty similar, had the same outlook on life and we were both bang into fanny and shagging. Obviously we are both good-looking blokes, so there was always competition between the two of us when we went out – all in good nature though. If I had two birds and he had none, he'd be well pissed off. Not just cos of competition, but cos he'd want a shag! But we never had to impress or prove anything to each other. I knew what he was capable of. I admired his skills. I saw how lasses looked at him and how they'd rush to his side in a club. And he could see that they did the same to me. So it was never a case that one had something over the other. That's why we teamed up and created the Buck Squad. What a belta!

I think with me willy! It runs off instinct. It's like a pneumatic drill.

Looking back, the two of us used to shag so much. We had some wild times, threesomes, foursomes, the lot. The foursome actually came about by accident thanks to a pissed-off Charlotte! Gaz and I had come back from a night out with these two girls and Charlotte wasn't happy with Gaz, even though she had a boyfriend. She was trying to be the ultimate cockblocker by interrupting him in his stride while he was getting busy in the shag pad. Gaz got so pissed off with her that he grabbed his lass, dragged her up to our room and got into bed with us. The result? An unplanned foursome. By the end of it Gaz and I were high-fiving over the girls, oi oi!

Gaz and I were like a double act for me first few seasons and the rest of the house joked that we were actually in love with each other. We probably were. But the thing is, we just got on so well and we loved going out together cos when we did hit the town we would encourage each other to have a cracking night.

We jokingly called ourselves the Buck Squad, but the girls got pissed off that we were pulling so much and just moaned all the time. They really wanted these fucking family nights in, eating pizza and stuff when all we wanted to do was graft birds and eat fanny. At one point the girls got so pissed off that they formed the Cockblock Crusaders to try to stop us from bringing lasses home. It was shit and it rarely worked.

While Gaz and I had hit it off and worked our way through the best girls Newcastle had to offer, the other newbie Dan was struggling to fit in. And we felt sorry him. For some reason he was finding it so hard to bag a bird. I dunno why, cos he was a good-looking lad, but I think he needed a bit more banter and confidence, and had to stop wearing them shit Voi jeans every night. I think he was a bit pissed off that Gaz and I got on so well and maybe he felt a bit left out sometimes. It wasn't intentional, but when we were out we had one mission – to pull and buck.

I remember one night Dan actually did bring a girl back and jumped into the bed next to mine with her cos Gaz was busy in the shag pad. All Dan was doing was cuddling the lass. Meanwhile, the bird I had was literally going mad, screaming like she was having triplets in the bed. It was right next to their bed. I thought afterwards how awkward it must have been for them to hear this girl screaming like a banshee! I mean, she was screaming, 'I'm coming, I'm coming.' What a liberty! His bird probably wanted to get involved.

While the producers obviously loved all the sex action in the house, they did on occasion tell me to cut down on shagging – which is like telling SpongeBob not to have square fucking pants. Sometimes, I would get so carried away shagging that producers would have to sit me down and tell me to tone down some of what I was doing cos 'Scott, we're not making a porno.' I think this came after a night in the jacuzzi where I was slapping me dick off some girl's head while she was sucking me balls and I was looking at the camera with me thumbs up, just loving it. They also ordered me and Gaz not to pull on certain nights so that we could have real discussions with the rest of the house, which was normally them going on about how much we pull. Pointless!

People always ask how much of it is set up, but it really isn't. As you know, each 42-minute episode is cut down from hours and hours of footage and producers use the stuff that they know will entertain the fans. And what happens on screen happens for real. Producers may line up locations that we go to but the arguments and situations are all real. So when we're in the house we are pretty much left to ourselves, to run riot with a camera crew following us about.

The only time we would really see the production team would be in green screen moments; you know, those clips that are shot a while after what we are talking about has happened. So we'll go into this studio and they'll remind us of a certain scenario and we'll react to it. So they'll ask something like, 'Right, so when you all went go-karting ... give us a few lines about that ... did you think you would win? Who did you think would be shit?', and so on. Producers tend to edit the stories first and then ask us about the events so they know which bits they want us to comment on. But that also tends to give away how you are gunna appear in the final edit cos they are asking about specific things that have happened.

I think that's where people on the show have gone wrong in the past, when they start worrying about the way they come across on the telly. Especially the newest lot who have come in, who are really worried about what they are doing. And I think that's why many of them don't end up on the show for very long cos they try to act their part. They aren't being themselves and they worry about the way they will be perceived by the viewers at home. When you do that, people can see right through you and know you're faking it. I do whatever I do and people like it. I don't give a fuck what anyone thinks.

Well, I say that. But when the filming of me first season had finished, there was one person I was worried about. Ashleigh. It was only now that filming had wrapped that it dawned on me that there were things I was gunna have to explain ...

It might sound funny, but in the house you feel like you're removed from the real world. Nothing you do in the *Geordie*

Shore bubble feels real. But when you're out of it, you realise you have to face up to the consequences. And so once I got home, I told Ashleigh what had happened. She was fucking furious, of course, why wouldn't she be?! I think she felt embarrassed that what I was doing could be seen on TV by her friends and family. I apologised and told her that what I did on the show meant nothing and that it was just part of the programme, which it is! I said it wouldn't happen again and, eventually, after much persuasion, she began to come round. She never fully forgave me and she was never happy about the situation, but she stuck by me for a couple more series before we finally went our separate ways.

24

GEORDIE SHORE: THE NEXT GENERATION

I really enjoyed making the first few series of *Geordie Shore*; it was a great life experience and I really grew to love me housemates. I know it looked like we argued a lot on screen but don't forget those 42 minutes of action are carefully selected for your pleasure.

The rest of the time we have a blast and we forged some really strong bonds. We are just like a family of dysfunctional brothers and sisters. That said, if there was one thing that bugged me it was the mess of the house. As you may recall, I can be a bit OCD, so you can imagine how I must feel when the place looks like it's had dynamite launched inside! Now, I bet you'd think it would be the lads who were the muckiest bastards in the house, but it's actually the girls who are filthier. Honest, they are rotten. They leave dirty plates lying around, dirty knickers on the floor, eyelashes all over the fucking walls and that, piss stains on the carpet, not to mention on each other. I've never lived in such a shit hole.

I remember the time Vicky kicked off about how lazy Marnie was being in the house and ordered her to do the washing up. But Marnie was having none of it and stuffed the dirty plates in a big black plastic bag and shoved it under a chair. But Vicky was nee pushover. When she found the bag, she stormed into Marnie's room and emptied it all over her bed. Instead of learning her lesson, Marnie just stuck a blanket over it and slept in the spare bed next to it. It was fucking ILL!

Ah, Marnie, Marnie, Marnie. When she arrived in the house in season seven, I have to admit I thought she was fucking mint. She was stunning and just the type for me big pipe. Pretty, with long dark hair. Of course the minute I saw her I wanted to moose her all over cos she was another fresh face and she was propa fit. But as I got to know her more I started to get a few feelings for her and then I got it bad.

But the problem with us was I never knew where I stood with her. I got with her a couple of times, but she blew hot and cold like a fucking uneven kettle. Did she fancy me or did she not? I could never tell. Was she trying to make Gaz jealous? Who knew? It also didn't help that Holly still fancied me and was propa pissed off about Marnie walking in and stealing her man. Not that I was hers to steal in the first place, the radge packet.

Just for the record, I know Holly and I had banged a few times, but never once did I lead her on. And I think she knew that. In all the time we've been on the show, she never took me to one side and asked me to have a relationship with her, but I knew she liked me and the choppa. When you're in the house you do grow close to people, so it's only natural. The thing is, if she did have those strong feelings for me that was her choice. It wasn't me fault that I was irresistible, or didn't feel the same way. Cos if I don't, I don't. I couldn't pretend. It became clear that when me and Marnie were getting on, Holly was a bit upset. I wasn't trying to rub it in her face. I just wanted to try to get me warrior in Marns!

To make matters worse, the production team was obviously keen to drive a wedge between Gaz and me and kept pairing him up with Marnie on jobs and that. I could see that she liked him and that she was flirty with him (probably on the advice of the production team). And knowing Gaz, I knew that he'd fancy her too and that really sent me loopy.

For one, I was pissed off with production for playing around with me emotions. They knew I fancied Marnie and tried to cause trouble. I was also angry at Marnie cos I didn't know whether or not she liked me and I wasn't sure if I could trust Gaz with her.

Throughout the series, I did get with Marnie a couple of times but it became a bit of a nightmare and a head fuck. One minute she'd be like, 'I like you,' the next she'd be arguing with you.

All this confusion started to get to me. And the less I knew about what was going on, the more angry I became. Of course, I have always had a short fuse and there have been many times I have totally lost it in the house and just smashed the place up.

As you'll know if you watch *Geordie Shore*, I have walked out so many times. I remember there was one time – one you didn't see – where I got so pissed off I just legged it all the way home in a pair of shorts, that's it! Four miles across town bare-fucking-foot in the winter. The production team got in touch with Michael the next day, found us in me bed and persuaded me to go back.

I was pissed off with production for playing around with me emotions.

*

Me first two series were wicked and I'd been pretty laid back about everything. But by the show's sixth series in Australia – me third on the show – I started to crack and began kicking off a whole lot more. I dunno why but I was just getting more and more angry. But it was in series seven with Marnie that brought out the real anger and I think it started to scare people, oops.

Cos I had these feelings for the girl – the first time I had actually had feelings like this for a lass in the house – I couldn't deal with the idea of Marnie cracking on with Gaz. And every time production would set them up to go to 'work' I was fucking hitting the roof. But instead of talking about it, I just let it simmer. Bad idea. Cos one day it was gunna overflow . . .

And so when I would get pissed off, I'd remove meself from the situation and storm off out of the show. Of course, production got seriously annoyed with me cos they couldn't make the show if I kept taking off. In fact, they were so annoyed that I was ordered into a meeting with producers to get a good telling off from them. They said I had to cool down, that me behaviour just wasn't right and warned me that if I continued to smash the place up and run off all the time I was 'going to lose me position on the show'. Wow! If ever there was a wake-up call, it was THAT!

These days I have managed to calm meself down a hell of a lot. I'm not as bad as I was, cos now I can just take it in and deal with it. So instead of starting fights with people on the show I now just take me anger out on objects like doors, walls and fucking plants, punching holes through things to make meself feel better. Me hands have taken a beating but they're strong. Me knuckles look like the rocky mountains pure popping out everywhere, cos if I get angry I just dig a wall.

The thing I had with Marnie kind of phased out by the end of series seven, once I realised she was a nightmare. I was dealt the most crushing blow when I found out that the day after we stopped filming, Gaz had gone round to Marnie's house and banged her. I was propa furious cos one, I still kind of fancied Marnie and two, Gaz was me mate and he clearly didn't give a fuck about the lad code. In fact, I think I was probably more hurt that he hadn't come clean after it happened. If he had I probably wouldn't have been so arsed.

When I saw Gaz next, I squared up to him in the street and demanded to know why he did what he did and why he hadn't had the decency to tell me about it. He said that cos

Marnie and I had left the house as 'friends' he had every right to get in there if he wanted to. Well, mate, not according to the lad code! You never go near a bird your mate had feelings for unless you at least talk about it first. It's just the way it is. Gaz was such a tool sometimes and had been telling newbie Aaron that he should steer clear of Marnie to protect me feelings and then he goes and does that for himself instead. What a load of bollocks.

I shouldn't have been surprised by Gaz, though, cos I had been suspicious of Gaz's grasp of the lad code back in Australia. He'd gone out on the town on his own and picked up three lasses, and brought them back. Well done, Gaz, you've played a blinder. Except, hang on, mate, isn't one of those girls the one I was necking on with the night before?

As a firm believer in the lad code, I didn't waste any time in confronting Gaz and told him I was majorly pissed off with him. I said to him, 'Would I ever do that to you?' And he said that me lass was only with him cos the girl that he was interested in would only come if her mates came too. Fair play. I softened a little bit when he said that but it still didn't excuse his intentions. I was really pissed off cos I thought he would never do that to me. I know for sure that I wouldn't do that to him.

But don't get me wrong, I'm not slating him. Gaz is a top bloke and to this day is me best mate in the house, along with Aaron we're a trio now. I'm just saying that once or twice he has done something that I have not been happy with. If it hadn't been for him being on the show I probably wouldn't have had as much of a frisk as I've had.

One of me favourite memories with him was when we pissed off the girls (and James) so much in Australia with our relentless pulling that we were sent off to a mining town that was four and a half hours away from Sydney in the Outback, which is in the middle of fucking nowhere. When we were sent off in a car, we reckoned it was gunna be as fanny-free as a fucking monastery – we were gutted! But what do you know? We got to this town and decided to go for a pint in its only bar. Walking in it was all lads and about three girls and we somehow still managed to pull and buck two of them in these fucking huts we were staying in. Gaz said to me, 'I cannot believe we're in the middle of nowhere and we still manage to pull.' It was hilarious. We were so buzzing with ourselves that when it came to the green screens we went in boasting, 'Here, you could stick us two on the fucking moon, and we'd still be able to find a shag!'

The show has definitely changed a lot since I first started in it. People have come and gone. And it's always sad when someone leaves the house. Like when Vicky left, it was a shock, but I think she did the right thing. She was a huge character in the show, but she has done so well for herself. Winning *I'm A Celeb* was just amazing for her. Look what doors it has opened for her. She's presenting now, something which she has always wanted to do.

However, I have to admit, when someone leaves the house there is only a small change in the dynamics. If someone else is causing a bit of drama and you have all these big characters sticking their noses in you tend not to notice the ones who aren't there any more.

Charlotte's departure was a shock but she's a canny lass and she knows what she's doing and I think she's done the best thing cos things were getting too much for her, too. It will be strange not to have her on the show any more, like. She was like me stupid kid sister and I'll miss her funny ways and seeing her pissed, shitting herself. We'll have to see what the house is like without the Gaz–Charlotte dynamic. Even though they'd see other people it was always there lurking in the background, and I guess the viewers loved the will-they-won't-they crack. Who knows if they will end up together? They had that massive public spat about that interview Charlotte gave revealing she'd been rushed to hospital with an ectopic pregnancy while Gaz was in *Ex on the Beach*. I can see Gary's point. Why does she have to tell the world? She really could have kept that quiet as it is something that is so very personal. But what's done is done and we can all be friends again, although Charlotte keeps saying that it will never be the same again between them. Let's see what happens, cos I've heard it all before!

When one old face disappears new ones replace them. We have a sound bunch of loons in the show at the moment who have given the show a bit of edge. Chloe is a good lass. I mean, what is she on, though? I don't think she knows what's going on half the time. When she first came on the show I did what I always do and smashed her box! But – HOLD ON – that wasn't the first time that I'd been with her. I had actually pulled her years ago in a bar called Perdu, at mine and Jermaine's night. Dirtiz. I brought her back to mine with some of her pals for a party. And this other lad who's with us said to us, 'But I'm seeing her.' And I said, 'Sorry mate, she's been trying to wank me off all night.' And he said to her, 'Is this kid your lad?' And she said to him, 'We're not seeing each other, man.' And he said, 'Yes we are!' And then they ended up having a fuck-off massive argument outside and then he stormed off home and I took her to bed and popped it in her.

When Aaron joined the show in series eight I was propa buzzed. I knew him from back when we both lived in Kenton. We were both massive charvers but he had his group and I had mine. We'd always see each other in the parks or down at Whitley Bay. He is such a sound lad and we are just like brothers. We argue all the time about girls and everything else, but then we always make up straight away. Aaron came into the show at the right time and has fitted in amazingly.

I think Nathan is a good lad. When he first joined the show, I wasn't sure if he was gay – until he told me he fancied me and tried to suck me off. When people come in they wanna make an impact and will go out of their way to do it. It's hard to explain. They try to be the characters they think they should be. It's hard to develop a character like that if it's not really who you are, which is why I think I have done so well cos I am what I am, a fucking melon!

Marty is one of the newest housemates. I don't really know him, but he's just a kid. When he gets drunk, he's a total nightmare.

From what I heard, he'd always been a bit of a wannabe and was one of those guys I spoke about before – those twats whose only dream in life is to become a reality star! I have a mate who works on the bar scene and he remembers that before Marty was on the show he was like this Billy Big Bollocks type of guy. It was just after me first season on the show and Gaz and I and a few mates were in the VIP section of Tiger Tiger.

The place was bouncing and everyone was trying to get into the VIP area, but me mate David is on the door making sure not everyone gets through to the area to bother us. Then up rocks this kid Marty – and he was giving it large. And me mate said to him, 'You're not getting in, kid.' And he snapped back, 'Who are you?' And me mate hit back, 'Who the fuck are YOU? Get back down there or I'll flatten you!'

He was literally full of lip and we had a little bit of a frisk and then as he walked away he screamed at me pal, 'One day I'll be in there, one day I'll be on the show!' Then the next thing you know, he's on. He was so cocky, a propa little char-ver like I was. But once you get to know the lad he's actually got a heart of gold and has been through a lot of grief in his life, which explains why he is the way he is. I only found this out once I'd spoken to him properly, because I don't like to make judgements based on other people's opinions. You've just got a take him with a pinch of salt or you'll end up want-ing to snap his neck.

A lot of people on the club scene in Newcastle now really try so hard to get on the show, and I think the problem is that these days all the guys that do come into the show, trying to be a character, trying to be the new Gaz or the new Scotty T, saying they wanna shag more lasses and they will put us in our place, but they're not and they won't. They never can be. They just try and fail. I mean I love Kyle. I'd known him prior to *Geordie Shore* and he is a lovely lad. Sound as fuck with an amazing family. But when he arrived into *Geordie Shore* he thought too much about what was expected from the show. The whole thing with Holly, where she told him she loved him, he thought too much and it ended up ruining it for him. He's quit the show now after the birthday series, or so you think . . .

It's a shame Chantelle left the show earlier this year cos she was totally radge. She's mates with some of me mates but I didn't know her that well. She's apparently been at one of me houses for a party before, but then again so has every other fucker in Newcastle (I'd never met her). When she walked in – again, fresh meat for Scotty T – what do you know, I wanted to blast her there and then. But I never did, she's just a tease. In fact, she teased me for that long that when I finally got a Thomas Tank (wank) I lasted about ten seconds. Chantelle says she left cos she wanted to be with her boyfriend, but I know she was always worrying about how she came across on the telly. She shouldn't have left.

I don't wanna blow me own trumpet but I've not changed at all since the day I walked in. I just do what I do. I am a right slag sometimes, I do go beserk and kick off, I do do stupid things. But I haven't got a bad heart! I just do what I do and fucking enjoy it. And I think people like me for it, at least I hope so, haha. I'm not trying to pretend to be someone

223

I'm not – there's no point. People say I get away with a lot and if anyone else said what I say about shagging birds everyone would think they were a pervert, but it's just me. It's just the way I am. I'm not lying: it's the law of gravity that if I go out, girls are all over us. It's not me fault! SOZ!

25

PAs and Making Celeb Pals

If I ever wanted to have a private life, I had well and truly fucked it up by joining the cast of *Geordie Shore*. The show was a monster. Rating well over a million viewers on MTV each week, its young fanbase is insanely loyal. Within an hour of me first episode airing me Instagram and Twitter followings went through the roof and I had messages from young girls telling me how much they fancied me and that I was their hero. I was buzzing.

Friends and family messaged me to say they thought I was great and was a brilliant addition to the show. Me mam said she was proud of us, even though she said she probably wouldn't watch any more episodes, and even me dad said, 'Good effort, son. It's about time you got paid for being an arsehole!' Better than nothing, I guess. Old friends from school, who I hadn't seen or spoken to in years, suddenly started sending messages of congratulations and when I was out total randomers came up to me to say hi and ask for a picture. I was like, 'EH?'. Life, I realised, was never gunna be the same again, but I felt like I was gunna enjoy it.

I was still the same Scotty T as I was yesterday. I hadn't changed one bit. I still had the same friends, still lived in the same house with me pals and I still wiped me own arse. It was other people who saw me differently but I could live with that.

Now I was considered by some as a celebrity, I found meself being asked along to flashy events and premieres and to do interviews for TV shows and magazines.

It was canny surreal, but exciting. It was amazing to see how appearing on a TV show could make you suddenly more interesting to people you had never met before.

Life, I realised, was never going to be the same again.

We may not have been filming *Geordie Shore* at that moment, but the hard work was really beginning to kick in once it was on air. Cos the show was so incredibly popular, me and the other cast mates were in big demand, especially from club managers around the country who wanted us to come to their venue to make a personal appearance. It was amazing how much they were willing to pay for someone like me to turn up on a night just to say a few words, take a few pictures, then go back to the hotel and probably buck some rascal. Of course, with me background in bars and clubs I understood how a personal appearance could boost takings significantly in a night, so was more than happy to take part.

226

Me PAs themselves are pretty formulaic. I would say they're different to a lot of other celebrities' PAs: the usual celeb would turn up about midnight, say a few words (if the club's lucky), participate in an event or be asked to judge some kind of contest and then spend an hour doing a meet-n-greet where they'd say hello and take photos with people. Mine, on the other hand, went like this: I'd turn up, either by meself or with me pals, start downing loads of drinks and going radge, entertain the crowd on stage, mc'ing on the mic and diving about half naked … I WAS IN ME FUCKING ELEMENT. Me meet-n-greets wouldn't end. Instead of just a quick hello and a photo, I was necking on with every bird, having banter with groups of lads and generally going beserk. I couldn't quite get the fascination with me. I was just a daft cunt from Newcastle, but I took full advantage and the clubs loved it. I was pretty stunned by the reactions. I had expected to have around 50 people come and see me. But in most cases I've had 800 people or more. I really can't believe the attention I have received from these people. It was fucking nuts. And all cos of what? Getting me cock sucked on TV!

Although doing PAs can be exciting and a lot of fun, they can also be pretty exhausting. One a week is fine, but I tend to get booked up almost every fucking night all over the country and even abroad. So, for example, on a Friday I could be appearing at a club in Sheffield and finish up around 4 a.m. Then me next PA would be in Aberdeen at 10 p.m., so I'd get the train, then I'd be up at the crack of dawn to get a flight to Italy from Edinburgh, have a four-hour drive from the Italian airport to some random club were no one speaks

English, then travel for four hours back to the airport early the next day followed by a flight to somewhere like Ireland on the Sunday before flying home Monday. I have to spend hours and hours in cars, trains, planes. Never a bus though. Fuck that! I'm no diva but I wouldn't dare be part of the Mega Bus brigade. You see, it can be boring and tiring especially if you've been balls deep all night!

When I first started out on the circuit I used to bring me mates along for moral support. They jumped at the chance as they knew they could reap the benefits – no club entry fee, free drinks and lots of attention from girls. What more could they ask for? However you have to choose which of your friends you bring along wisely. Otherwise, if they're crackers, it could be a disaster.

I did an appearance at a Harlem Shake party in Leeds a couple of years back for me mate Dave at a club called Oceana, and brought along four of me mates, including me stripper mate Adam. I had been asked by the club to go up on stage to get the crowd whipped into a massive frenzy. And as the crowd started jumping around, me mate Adam jumps up on stage with me, whips all his clothes off and flashes his cock for everyone to see. Although I am pretty used to Adam doing this, I didn't expect him to flash his knob at a club I was actually working at! Wafting his big pipe around the stage in front of 1,000 students.

While most of the girls in the room appeared awestruck by Adam's eel swinging from side to side like a pendulum, the club management were not as impressed and put in a complaint to me agent. I later had to remind me mate that if

I invite him to any future PAs he has to behave himself! This happened all the time with different mates, because like me, they are all loose fuckers.

But it's not just tanked-up friends who can be a problem when I'm on the road; sometimes I can lose control of meself.

Back in 2014, I was doing a personal appearance at a nightclub in Rhyl, North Wales. It started off like any other night; I met fans, had a load of pictures taken, and enjoyed the odd neck here and there with the local fanny. But as the night progressed, things started to change. I'm used to being surrounded by lots of people all wanting photos, girls grafting me, and the odd lad pecking me head about becoming me new best mate, but for some reason, on this night, the club seemed to get busier and busier and I started to feel more and more hemmed in by the swarms of people. The air-con was fucked and it was boiling. I started to feel quite intimidated by the mass of people surrounding me. Stupidly, I grabbed a full bottle of tequila and downed the whole thing. All of a sudden this guy starts prodding and grabbing me neck. I have no idea what the fuck he is doing and all I can think about is that this kid is getting a bit hostile and he keeps grabbing me neck. So what I do? I punch him straight in the head. The minute I did it I knew I had made a mistake. I had snapped, like I do sometimes, but the gimp deserved it at the time. Now I look back and think there was probably a better way to handle it, haha! I had to go to court where I owned up to me mistake and was punished with a fine.

Me personal appearances are not just restricted to the UK. A lot of me work is in Australia, where *Geordie Shore* is ridiculously popular. They can't get enough of us apparently and are super keen that we come visit their clubs and events as often as possible. Among me favourite bookings are the Schoolies, which are like the Aussie equivalent of fresher's week but for the 17-, 18- and 19-year-olds who have just finished their last year of school. Like Spring Break in Cancun, hundreds of young and up-for-it students descend on hotels around the Gold Coast to go fucking mental, even though it's officially a booze-free event.

When I head over there I always get a great response from the fans. I've been told that you only tend to be booked if you're popular on the show but I've noticed that if you're one of the guys in a relationship, you don't get booked that often either. Promoters always say they want the ones who will go out and party and have a fucking good time. And I have actually had promoters book me for a PA who have got more fucked than me, cos they're that buzzing to actually just have a drink and a laugh with you, but can never handle it. Cos Australia doesn't get as many acts coming over, with it being so far away, the organisers treat you really well over there, you feel like pure royalty.

Like a normal PA, I'd usually go up on stage and chat to the crowd a little and try to get them to go wild. The kids must be on something cos whatever you say, they'll start cheering. Sometimes you feel like a member of One Direction! It's the next level!

Of course, as Australia is such a vast country, moving from one city to the next can be a pain. When I moaned earlier about the four- or five-hour journey from Sheffield to

Aberdeen, it's a picnic compared to the five-hour flight from Melbourne to Perth. Cos of that and the ferocious heat, you end up so knackered.

I also have a monthly residency PA in Magaluf during the summer. A lot of the people who go to holiday destinations like that tend to be big fans of the show. Most are on their first lads, or lasses, holiday, propa revved up for a laugh, so these PAs are propa mint. There was one class summer in 2013 when I was booked to appear alongside the gorgeous Sam Faiers from *TOWIE*. We were hosting a hilarious North vs South competition – I would get a northern lad out of the crowd and she would pull up a sexy Southern lass and we'd have to set them various challenges to see who could do stuff best. Of course the challenges weren't particularly brainy, they were more about trying to get the pair of them naked – which they pretty much did without too much persuasion.

Sam was a beauty and a good laugh and totally under-stands this crazy world she is in and we had great banter on stage.

On the subject of star names, there have been so many rumours about me and Ellie Goulding and that we're dating. Well, we're not. I think she's fucking gorgeous, but we just have a great friendship and I've been to a couple of her shows. I took a couple of me pals along to her London gig at the O2 and got to chill backstage with her and her mates John Newman, the lads from Bastille, and Niall Horan. It's times like this when I know I've come a long way from being that little radge kid bouncing eggs off car windscreens. Once upon a time I used to be one of those thousands of people in the arena watching big music stars like Ellie doing their thing on stage. Now I'm hanging out with them backstage and having a sound night with them. They're just like me: down to earth and a good crack!

A few weeks later, I returned the favour. When Ellie was playing in Newcastle I promised I would take her out and get her mortal. So me and Jermaine took her, her manager and her crew to our night, Dirtiz. Even though it's a bit mental in the club at our night, she propa loved it so much that she was on the radio and said she'd had so much fun and that I was 'amazing and so funny'. Cheers, Ellie, wink wink!

Oh, did I forget to mention that one of the pals I took to Ellie's show in London was me stripper mate Adam? And yes, you're right; the twat did rip off all his clothes again, in front of everyone. Oh Adam, you fucking clown egg!

26

WAKE-UP CALL

'Hi Scott, can you call me please, we need to talk ... I'm pregnant.'

I had just played back a random voicemail from earlier in the day and couldn't believe what I was hearing; I thought she was having a laugh.

Pregnant? Is she off her barnet?! Did I actually just hear what I thought I did, the word pregnant? I replayed the voicemail from the girl – who I'll call Simone – to make sure I wasn't tripping.

'Hi Scott, can you call me please, we need to talk ... I'm pregnant.'

Nope, I heard it right. A girl saying she's up the DUFF.

I literally shit a breeze block, me body frozen and me heart pounding. I wasn't sure what to believe. Who the hell was this Simone, like? I couldn't for the life of me place her ... it was scrambling me brain.

What scared me the most is that I had saved her number

into me phone – which is normally me way of remembering if I've slept with a girl or not. I'd either save their number or add them on Facebook or summat, just in case I ever needed to get hold of them in the future for the rematch.

I immediately started checking the full works: Instagram, Facebook – even fucking Bebo – to try and find out who this cracker was, but couldn't find any sign of a Simone, like. But the fact I had saved her number in the first place made me balls disappear with worry, cos I most likely wouldn't have saved this number unless something had happened between us. What the fuck was going on? Madness, bro!

There was only one way to find out. I had to call her back.

I pressed the callback button and it rang out. And rang out. It was ages before she picked up and then . . .

'Hello, it's Simone . . .' the voice on the other end said, with a thick Northern Irish accent (thought it was a fucking lad for a minute, haha). 'You got me message then.'

Northern Irish, hmmm. The voice sounded slightly familiar, but then I had met lots of Northern Irish girls over the past year.

'What you on about?' I asked, 'Is this true?' I listened to her story to see whether she was full of shit and if there was a way I could catch her out.

Unfortunately, her story was legit. I was where she said I was on the date in question, and she told me where I'd entered the dragon. It sounded very familiar indeed.

I asked what she wanted from me. She umm'd and aah'd for a minute and said she didn't want anything from me and assured me that she wasn't trying to trap me into anything.

She said she had felt that it was only right to let me know that she was pregnant and that she wasn't gunna go through with it. Forgive me for saying it, but the sudden relief I experienced when she said that she wasn't planning on keeping the baby was overwhelming, cos I knew for sure that I wasn't ready to be a dad. I had enough trouble looking after meself, never mind a mini Scotty T. Fucking hell!!

We both continued to discuss the situation a bit more and by the end of the conversation, I told her I would fly her over to Newcastle to sort things out, as it's still not possible to have the procedure in Northern Ireland. I thought it was the right thing to be with her when she went through with it.

As I hastily made arrangements for her visit, I still wondered whether or not I could really believe what this girl was telling me. After all, people lie all the time, they talk shit saying they've got with me, or make stuff up like a fake pregnancy, just to get attention. I say hello to a girl nowadays and the next thing I'm engaged! Rumours spread like wildfire, especially in Newcastle. Also, if she was really pregnant, who's to say the baby was actually mine, unless we did a DNA test, like on *Jezza Kyle*. There was a lot to think about.

I knew for sure that I wasn't ready to be a dad.

But, after much thought, and basing me decision on the details she had given me, I felt inclined to believe her, even more so cos she had called me directly first and not, like so many people could have done, run to a newspaper to sell her

235

'I'm pregnant with Scotty T's baby' exclusive. That actually spoke volumes to me. If she was an opportunist, she could have tried to make way more money by selling her story to a tabloid instead of calling me; creeps do it all the time. Anyways ... So I believed this bird and thought it was only right to stand by her and help her take the next step.

When fucking Simone (nah man, let's be nice) – when Simone arrived in Newcastle a few days later, I did actually recognise her, but I only had a hazy recollection as I was off me lips the night I'd stuffed her. She was pretty, like, just me type (which is everyone, in case you hadn't noticed), so the kind of girl I quite possibly could have shagged. She seemed very sweet, very normal and didn't give off any of the gold digger vibes. Me gut instinct told me that she was genuine. And all the time she was with me she never asked for anything out of the ordinary, she never struck me as someone with an agenda. In fact she was very quiet, very nervous and I felt sorry for her.

I accompanied her to the clinic where everything was taken care of quickly and sensitively and then I drove her back to the airport, closing the door on that episode once and for all. To be honest it was the only occasion this had happened, despite the amounts of fanny I've had. But I dealt with it properly and respectfully, as should anyone else in that situation, FYI.

I never heard from Simone again and I will probably never know for sure if the baby was mine. But I couldn't take the chance that it was. Don't get me wrong, I'm not a nasty person at all; it's all fun and games until something like this becomes real, but I had to be mature and think about what was best for her and best for Scotty T. If there was a chance that she was carrying me baby I was never gunna leave this poor girl struggling on her own, that's not right. She'd been adamant that she wasn't keen to have the baby, and just needed me help to sort things out in England . . .

The baba bombshell certainly came as a wake-up call, like, and really made me stop to think (for about 15 minutes) about how careless I have been over the years. Then I just cracked on. I know part of me *Geordie Shore* schtick is to boast about the amount of women I have slept with over the years (which is loads), but this really made me sit up and take stock of how responsible I have been and should be in the future and that I am lucky to have had just the one person come forward with a pregnancy scare.

This also pointed out to me just how lucky I've been over the years. Yes, there have been times when I've been stupid and haven't wrapped me tool because a lot of the times I sleep with girls it's a random unplanned scenario (one-night stand) and I've either been drunk, in a rush or the fucker has split cos of me sheer girth. Sometimes I get girls saying daft things to me like, 'you must be riddled!' or 'I'm not sleeping with you – who knows what diseases you have!' In all fairness I understand why they might think this due to me behaviour on TV and me reputation as an international pipe master. But the actual truth is, despite me high number of sexual encounters, I am clean as a fucking whistle. There has been one occasion where I got checked up when I was about 19 and ended up with chlamydia, but I knew straight away who I'd got it off as the previous week I'd got so drunk I ended up shagging some dirty arse bird, so I wasn't that surprised that I'd caught the clap. What with me OCD, I am always so conscious of me body and looking after it. If I think there is the slightest chance I might be rocking an STD I will go and get checked out immediately. Better safe that sorry, crew!

*

Although this has been me only pregnancy scare, the other side of me reputation from *Geordie Shore* is that I get girls telling me all the time that I have supposedly slept with their mates, when their mate is just clearly taking shit to try and look cool. The most common one is bumping into random groups of lasses I don't know:

'Scotty T, you shagged our mate, Steph!' they'll say to me.

And I'll be like, 'But I have never met any of you before. I dunno who you are!'

'But you have, she told us,' they'll say.

And I'll say, 'Show us a picture.' I'll look. 'No I haven't.'

'Yes you have!'

So I'll say, 'Areet then, I tell you what, ring her right now and put me on the phone.'

And they'll ring her up and I'll be like, 'Oi, oi, is this Steph? This is Scott. Apparently you've slept with me?'

The girl is always pretty embarrassed, while her friends chorus in the background: 'Yes you did, you *told us* you did.'

To Steph: 'Please stop telling people you have slept with me when you know you haven't. Bye.'

And then to her mates: 'However girls, you would know if

238

I had slept with her cos she'd be walking like a fucking lobster.'

People do it all the time and I have to keep proving them wrong, which gets very frustrating and can often cause problems with current girls. But I know now that it's all part of being in the public eye. You have to take the head blags. But please girls, stop lying, it's boring. And watch out lads cos some people will do anything for a bit of fame these days. It's shocking.

You see, if I have a girl on social media or I have her number then I have probably shagged her. If not, then I *know* I haven't. You see, for security, I will always take a number or add them to social media in case I ever need to get in touch with them for any reason. I always make sure I know who they are. I mean the girl who phoned me up about being pregnant – I couldn't remember shagging her to start with, but cos I had her stored in me phone it was a definite sign that I might have been with her. I know it's not the most convincing way of confirming hooking up with someone, but it's the way I've always done it.

Of course, living in the public eye I expect these kind of things to crop up from time to time. And for every good thing I experience from being famous, I know there will always be a bad one.

One of the worst experiences I have had to deal with was when I did an interview with a newspaper in which a private matter I touched on was blown into a sensationalistic headline, which not only upset me but me whole family.

During the chat I had been asked why I was going away to

Australia and I told the reporter that one of me relatives wasn't well and that me family and I were going out to see her cos she'd been given a time limit and I wanted to spend as much time with her as I could. I specifically told the reporter (before and after the interview) that I didn't want the story about me relative to be out there, and politely asked the reporter if they'd mind not including the story about me sick family member cos it was so very personal, which they agreed to.

The next thing I know I see the headline: 'Scotty T Flies to Australia to See Dying Auntie!'

This was fucking ridiculous as the whole interview was supposed to be about *Geordie Shore*, so it didn't make sense. I was fucking foaming cos I had specifically and politely asked the reporter not to mention her in the paper cos it was personal family shit. I was so angry. And I was so shocked at how snide some reporters could be.

The worst part was that me family, who were dealing with the fact that their loved one was gravely ill, had to see it splashed across a newspaper and then all over the internet. It wasn't nice for them; in fact it made it worse. It makes me wonder what goes through people's heads when they are publishing stuff like this. I know these people have to sell papers and have to use eye-catching headlines, but do they ever think how insensitive something like that might be to a family who aren't in the public eye going through a lot of personal shit?

That story hurt me and me family a lot and I felt like I wanted to track down this reporter and have them shot – or at least make them experience the pain they had caused us. It's all well and good writing about me, I have put meself out there, write what you like. But me family aren't part of the game and haven't asked to be in the spotlight and shouldn't be forced into it – especially when they were going through such a terrible time.

27

It's Complicated

With the show still such a big part of me life, finding true love was never really something I was after. And yet, whenever I went out I would meet girls who I really fancied and got on well with. But that's all there could be to it. A quick neck, a buck or two and maybe some nights in with cuddles and *Family Guy*, but that's it. I'd learnt from experience that trying to have a relationship in the public eye is tough cos people always just wanted to get involved in me business.

This proved to be very hard for me and the girl in question, so most of the time, without getting too caught up, I would be completely honest with them, saying (without sounding too crude) that most likely it's only ever gunna be a shag or a neck on. It's better to be honest cos at the end of the day, me job is to party on TV, spending five weeks at a time away from home without mobile phones or contact with the outside world. If I was to go into a relationship it wouldn't be fair for either of us as I would wanna spend every day with that girl, not just certain periods of the year. And they wouldn't exactly enjoy watching me going beserk on *Geordie Shore*. So yes, a lot of the times I've ended up sacking off a lot of these birds – not in a bad way though, I'm never nasty. It's cos I think it's best for everyone if we just look at the whole situation and take on board that it wouldn't exactly be healthy for both of us to fall in love, cos I know I'm not in a position to fully commit to a relationship. We're only young, man!!

Me job and the workload it brings with it means I couldn't physically do it, not just cos I wanna shag about. And when I do develop feelings for a girl, despite the honesty it becomes harder and harder.

Then in June 2015 something strange happened . . . I met a girl who was different, someone who was more than a quick shag, a lot more! Someone I looked at and thought, 'Fuck me, she is marriage material!' But, of course, with me commitment to *Geordie Shore*, it was complicated.

So there I was out drinking one Monday night at the House of Smith in Newcastle with a bunch of mates. I was scanning the room as I do for some fit birds to stuff, when I suddenly caught sight of this sensational-looking girl in a white halter-neck top and a pair of pale blue jeans. She had long dark hair that was in loose curls and she was an absolute diamond. Nee word of a lie, I fell in love with her (and her arse) that very second.

Now, as you know, I don't ever get nervous about girls, but for the first time, I did feel a little bit funny. There was something different about this rascal. She looked like no other girl I had ever seen before; she was so beautiful and so classy that she pure shit all over all the other girls I'd been with before.

I really wanted to go over and crack on but it took a while. I felt a bit fucking shy for some reason, haha! I think probably cos I was knew this girl was gunna be hard graft and I knew I'd seen her as more than just a ride. So I got me mate Jed, who sort of knew her, to go over and speak to her for me. I felt like I was 13. He went over and went 'Me mate fancies you' (like you would in a school fucking disco). I know it sounds pretty textbook school boy but I didn't wanna scare her off with me over-confident charms. I knew exactly how I needed to play it. I was so worried that if she knew who I was, me reputation might frighten her away. Anyways, Jed went over and I glanced over every now and then to see what was going on:

FRANCESCA: So this guy came over and told me his 'friend fancied me'. I laughed at him and looked over at Scott who was wearing this black velvet waistcoat! 'We're not in school,' I said. 'Tell your friend he can come and tell me instead.' So we called him over and Scott was kind of shy and cute and not as cocky as most people know him to be. I was so drunk I started to pretend I was a cat, don't know why, but I did. I was stroking him, I was purring and meowing all night. He kept on trying to chat me up and all I did was meow at him and lick my hands like they were paws. It was ridiculous; I don't know why he liked me at all.

244

So it turned out that her name was Francesca. She was 21, from Consett and was a model and lifeguard! Like Newcastle's answer to Pamela Anderson! Anyway, I worked me magic on her while she pretended she was a cat all night and then I invited her and her mates back to mine for a party. Only when I got back to me Quayside pad, I realised I was fucking locked out. So, tanked up as I was, I tried to scale the back wall via this drainpipe, only the wall was about 20 feet high and as smooth as me cock. I was having nee luck; meanwhile all the drink and balloons me mates had ordered to the house had arrived. We were then stuck outside drinking and getting rowdy! I then started trying to kick me front door through but seriously failing. I was so desperate to get to know this bird before the night ended. I was going mad. It was a fucking liberty. Luckily Francesca obviously liked us back and suggested that we all go back to her student accommodation.

When we got there we had a gaff and I ended up staying as I still couldn't get into me pad but Fran was so drunk she kept on falling out of the bed, so we didn't have sex (not that we would have anyways as I could tell she was different). Then we joined the others in the living room and pushed the couches together to make a studio box and had a mad party with our mates.

When we woke up the next morning there were just three of us left: me, Fran and me mate Tilly, who we found wedged down the side of the sofa in this box student room! I woke up and left her sleeping for a little bit. She was every bit as gorgeous as she was the night before. When she woke up and went to the loo, I grabbed her phone and punched in me number. After she dropped me off at home, I thought to meself, 'Wow, she is something else!' As I watched her drive off I knew I just had to see her again! I wouldn't let her get away, like.

FRANCESCA: No sooner had I dropped him off than my phone started ringing. I picked up my phone and the caller ID said 'Scotty Lush Cock xxxxxxxx'. I couldn't help but laugh. What a sweetie. He told me he had had a great time and that he wanted to see me again. I was chuffed cos I really liked him too. The next day he phoned me again to tell me he was taking me out and picked me up in his mate's BMW an hour later and took me to Spy Bar in Jesmond, where five or six of his lad mates were waiting. I felt so weird, it was broad daylight and I hadn't had a drink yet. But his mates thought we were similar and that I was very confident and they loved the fact that we trying to outdo each other with our funny stories.

From then on we were inseparable and saw each other every day. It was really light-hearted and Francesca had told me that she had just got out of a four-year relationship and wasn't looking for anything too serious, which was music to me ears!

We kind of became girlfriend and boyfriend, but Francesca said from the start that she didn't like the idea of being written about in the press, which made me happy cos it meant that she wasn't some starfucker trying to get a step up into telly.

Now here is where it got complicated. On paper, Francesca was everything I wanted in the perfect woman. She was stunning, funny and she necked pints. What more could a lad want? But cos of me role on *Geordie Shore*, there was just no way I could commit to her and give her what she wanted. Also with the way things were workwise I would never be around enough for her to see me and, as I'd learnt from the past, that really doesn't help a relationship.

But the thing was, I propa liked her, maybe even loved her and I didn't wanna lose her. I was in a total fucking dilemma. It was like a case of choosing between the show and me personal life. I was 27 at the time and I knew I was reaching an age where lads like me start looking around for that special person to settle down with and firing out kids. And it is something I wanna do. One day! But also I felt that I was still starting out me career and cos of the nature of the show I am part of, being single and being able to carry on being the wild party boy the show sees me as was important.

It was going to be strange now working on these shows knowing that I had someone special in me life.

I sat her down and explained that as long as I was on *Geordie Shore* I had to live a certain way on the telly. I told her that I was at a stage in me life where I was making lots of money and it was still me time to shine. I was doing so based on what people liked about me when they watched me on the show. I was Scotty T, the insane party animal, who everyone loves. Playing that part – which was really just an extension of me – was me bread and butter at that moment, and I still have more dreams and aspirations.

Then I dropped the next bombshell – that I had been signed up for *Ex on the Beach*, MTV's other popular reality show about a bunch of sexy young boys and girls living together in a villa, who invariably shag each other before their exes suddenly make a shocking appearance.

I was genuinely worried about Fran's reaction cos I wanted to keep seeing her but she took me by surprise and was very understanding indeed. She was so chilled out and said to me, 'I know what your job is, and I don't want to change you. Do the show, I'm not going to stop you.' I was thrilled. How perfect was this girl? She was fit and lovely and everything I could ask for but she also understood how important the show was to me. Wow! What a result.

She also said to me that she had heard of some people who had left shows like *Geordie Shore* to be with their boyfriends or girlfriends and had been forced to go back to their ordinary lives. She said to me she didn't wanna be responsible for me quitting me career and ending up like them. I was thrilled.

Although our relationship would be a bit strange as a result, I was pleased that I had met a girl who I had genuine propa feelings for but who understood the weird predicament I was in cos of me job. Of course, it was gunna be strange now working on these shows knowing that I had feelings for someone special in me life, but I couldn't let that affect me. I am Scotty T and people love me for who I am. There was no way I could suddenly be celibate Scotty; there would be no way of explaining it cos Francesca wouldn't be on the show because of her career. So how could I explain on telly a girlfriend who I couldn't show to everyone? People just wouldn't buy into it and then I'd be out of a job. And I needed to continue to make money! There were so many things I wanted to do and it wasn't the right time to fuck it all up.

But to have Francesca onside was a bonus and was definitely a weight off me shoulders before I set off to Portugal to film series four of *Ex on the Beach*, which, as it would turn out, proved to be a tough few weeks of filming emotional highs and lows.

28

Ex on the Beach

When I was offered the chance to appear on *Ex on the Beach*, I didn't think twice. Three weeks away in Faro, Portugal living with a bunch fit girls sounded like paradise. So I said, 'Ow, fucking yes sir!'

Unlike the previous series, which were quite tame, when the celebs usually drop into the villa as the 'exes', I was being brought in as one of the original eight. Now, I knew from the outset that the show is designed to stitch you up. The producers might want you to shag the girls in the villa but then when you least expect it, they drop in someone's ex. I knew what to expect, and I knew I would have an ex or two suddenly rock up to fuck up me world. But hey, I'm Scotty T and I am a grand master of handling this kind of thing. I know every trick in the book – I might as well have written the fucking thing.

The way I looked at it was I had an advantage over the others cos I had TV experience while the others hadn't. Being in front of a camera comes second nature to me so I felt pretty at home. And while I was more relaxed and natural on camera, I noticed over the course of the three weeks how desperate the others were to be famous. It's sad, cos you see a lot of people hoping it can turn them into a big star by trying to be something they're not. I went on just being me and rocked yet another show! They might as well as have called the show *Scotty T on the Beach*!

The cast were all gorgeous. I don't think there was a girl in there I wouldn't have rooted and the fellas were all sound too, although a few of them went on like divvies. I soon put them in their place!

When I clocked Olivia, straight away I thought she was areet cos she had a propa dirty face on her! It was a lustful thing with her. I knew I just wanted to pump the arse off her. But it turns out she was wicked at giving blowjobs too. Hold tight. She sucked me off on the first night. We'd gone on a date straight from the beach on a yacht and she kept telling me she didn't do anything on a first date – an hour or two later she was playing me cock like a fucking plunger. Yeah, good one for playing the waiting game, pet. Sadly me plans to buck her all trip were ruined when her ex James arrived the next day. He was a handsome lad but a cocky twat and full of shit. He was pissed off when he heard that she had got with me. But I didn't give a fuck cos I didn't know him and it was her decision to get with me. If I was in that situation I wouldn't have been pissed off with the lad cos it's not his fault. It was the girl's fault as usual, haha!

Youseff was a guy I had met previously in Cancun when

I was on holiday with me lads. From what I remember he had been a sound guy who was pretty chilled. But now in front of the camera he was all lairy and 'Oh, hey Scotty!'

Nancy May was fit. Pretty face, long dark hair. And I shagged her eventually after she played hard to get, for all of five minutes. All was looking good with her until another girl called Lacey arrived on the island – and I started shagging her too. It became a bit of a sticky situation between the two cos I kept going from one to the other and they weren't happy about it. After I told Nancy that I liked her, I ended up sleeping with Lacey again when she gave me the cold shoulder. It was pretty fucked up! But hey, we were on a TV show.

This other guy, Lewis, was brilliant. He was a very natural guy but a bit of a handful, and appeared as though he didn't care about the programme he was on. I'm telling you, he was total nuts. He got into loads of fights and he didn't like people who were rude. When Olivia's ex arrived on the island he thought the way he treated her was disgraceful and squared up to him to tell him off. His downfall on the show came when Megan McKenna and her soon-to-be fiancé Jordan arrived on the island and he told Megan that he thought she was the type of girl he'd like to marry. Of course, that went down like a shit sandwich with Jordan after Megan did a bit of stirring. It all kicked off, they started fighting and Lewis got chucked off the show when he smashed up a few chairs and got wrestled to the ground by security. Liberty!

The other housemates were pretty sound too and we had some really fun nights together, when it wasn't kicking off! We would normally be alerted to the arrival of an ex when the tablet of terror – the iPad that give us instructions – pinged. Then three of us would go down to the beach and await the arrival of a mystery guest. For the first few days, I got off Scott(y) free. But then eventually me day came, and who should stroll out of the ocean but me ex Ashleigh Defty. Fucking liberty!!

I knew of all me exes it would be Ashleigh who would probably turn up cos a lot of me other exes wouldn't be bothered about being on TV. It was nice to see her, cos obviously we had been very much in love, but that moment was way gone now so I didn't have that interest any more. Besides, she and Olivia's ex James seemed to have eyes for each other and started shagging – when he could get it up, that is.

While I was away from the cameras I would occasionally FaceTime Francesca to assure her everything was fine and to tell her I loved her. Of course, I didn't tell her that I had been bucking girls on the island but I didn't say I hadn't either. I had shown me romantic side too cos while I was away Francesca celebrated her 21st birthday and I had arranged for a pair of Louboutins to be sent to her. She loved them apparently, but I bet she thought they were to make amends for something I'd done.

When Jordan proposed to Megan, Ashleigh was in tears cos it made her think that if we had stayed together that could have been us. (Er, NAR, I thought.) The next day the tablet of terror sent the two of us on a romantic date. It was a really lovely stroll around the grounds of this big house. Dotted around the location were some sentimental photographs of the two of us which were actually quite sweet. It did remind me that Ashleigh and I had had some good times. But in me head that was then and this was now. I did get the feeling that she might wanna get back with me, but I really wasn't arsed to be honest. At this point we were friendly, that was good enough for me. Although we had a silent kiss, I didn't try it on with her. I think after that date she started getting feelings again but I wasn't bothered. She was an ex for a reason.

I really enjoyed me three weeks on the show but I learnt one thing: that people who try out for these shows do get it wrong. I really think they try to be like people they've seen on other shows, and some of them think you can get a TV career just by copying something or someone you've seen. But they don't realise that this stands out a mile on the TV. Viewers can tell when someone's putting on an act. It's good TV if you believe that's what the people you are watching are really like, and they are reacting to everything that happens the way they would react in real life. If it's fake then it's not interesting any more.

Without blowing me own trumpet, I think people were pretty in awe of me on *Ex on the Beach* so no one tried anything with me cos they knew I'd shoot them down. I think that the others on the show didn't argue with me cos they liked me, but also cos they were worried how it would come across. But they didn't realise that if they had argued with me they would have come across a bit more naturally. They were just sitting there not saying anything, worried that arguing with me would make them look bad! But I say, do

what you do. I can tell within ten seconds of meeting someone what they are like. I know who I can trust. I knew what
the lads on the show were like. A lot of them packed in their
jobs after *Ex on the Beach* cos they thought they'd launch a TV
career. And I just thought, you've got the wrong train of
thought.

I was glad when the show was finally over: shagging and
arguing can really take it out of you. I was
also happy to get home and relax and
chill with Francesca. Nancy and Lacey
arguing over me had been a strain
and I got sick of both of them so
I just went off with Olivia in the end.
After we wrapped the show we had
to do some promo stuff for the series,
and while we were staying in the hotel
I shagged her on the bathroom floor while
Nancy was asleep in bed. But no one knows that! Ha!

I had to face up to the fact that I felt really guilty about what I'd got up to.

When I got back to Newcastle, I was feeling a bit blue cos
now I was away from the weird, parallel universe of the
show, I had to face up to the fact that I felt really guilty about
what I'd got up to. I knew I had to come clean to Francesca,
but wasn't sure how she'd react. We'd spoken briefly on the
phone and she asked me, 'Have you done anything?' and I
said 'no'. Feeling even worse now, I kept me distance for the
next week or so as I fought with the guilt I felt for sleeping
with the girls on the show. Then I couldn't bear it any longer
and I decided I had to tell her, as the series would be airing

255

soon anyway. So I met up with Francesca and broke down and said: 'Look, I did get with someone on the show, I slept with two girls. I'm really sorry.'

Francesca was great and said she understood why I had done what I had done and forgave me. She really is a mint lass. A one in a million.

After I did another *Geordie Shore* series, I took Francesca to Perth, Australia with me dad and family to visit his sister who was ill. We had a great time together, just chilling out and sleeping on the beach. It really was beautiful and I realised as I lay next to Francesca how lucky I was. But little did I know that there was a surprise waiting around the corner.

29

CELEBRITY BIG BROTHER CALLING

Having just finished filming *Ex on the Beach* and trying to piece me relationship with Francesca back together, I was looking forward to some time out. It was shaping up to be a big 2016 with a special birthday series of *Geordie Shore* planned as well as the two regular series. But then out of the blue *Celebrity Big Brother* came calling and asked if I fancied taking part in the 2016 series in January.

Now, I am always up for a challenge but *CBB* is one of those shows that can make or break you. So many stars have gone in loved by the public and come out totally ruined so it takes a very brave person to agree to sign up to it. Although, of course, I would always say that anyone who does come away hated by the public usually has him or herself to blame for having done something pretty radge, so I was thinking, 'I'm fucked'.

It was definitely a tempting offer cos a lot of people still talked about the show and it had proved to be a great way for people to raise their profile or to show the public a different side to themselves. As much as I loved *Geordie Shore*, I was really up for people to see that I wasn't just this bucking, shagging, banging fuck-monster. That I was also this funny, sensitive kid, too.

But could I do as well as our Charlotte who had won the show in 2013 in spite of pissing the bed? Vicky's ex Ricci came eighth a year later, but he was fucking shit, so no surprise. But then everything our cast touched these days seemed to turn to gold. Vicky had just been crowned Queen of the Jungle on *I'm a Celebrity* after the nation had seen a new side to her and had fallen in love with her. Could I do as well as that? Or would I end up being another Ricci G?! Fuck that, nee chance. There's no way I could be that shit, surely?!

All me doubts were forgotten when I heard what kind of ridiculous fee they were willing to offer for me (I don't like talking figures, but let's just say it was a lot). I thought to meself, 'Wahey man, where do I sign mateee?!'

But before anything was signed, I had to meet with the show's tough but very well-respected celebrity producers. You see, choosing the right mix of celebs isn't just coincidence. It takes a bunch of talented people to cast the right kind of varied and volatile characters to make the show work.

I met with Ros and Hannah in a café at the show's production company, Endemol, and even though I was hungover to fuck, I was buzzing like a bee. The girls didn't waste any time and fired a bunch of questions at me about *Geordie Shore*, who I would like to cast alongside me on the show ('fit birds' I think I said), who would I miss most ('me mam') and shit like that! I didn't try to impress them and show off, I was just me, said what I thought, and didn't give a shit. They seemed to like what I had to say cos both lasses – who were pretty mint – were pissing themselves laughing, which I took as a good sign. At the end of the meeting they said they'd be in touch and would let me know what they thought.

A day later me agent got the call from Hannah telling us that they had loved meeting me – I have that effect on women – and wanted me to be one of their cast! I was well chuffed, not just cos of the money and everything that came with appearing on the show but also cos it's always nice to know that someone has the confidence in you. When I later found out that Gaz had been in to see the girls as well but they had chosen me instead – well, that was just the icing on the cake! Top boy me, like!

When I told Francesca about me plans she was happy for me, but gutted that I was gunna be away again for a long period of time without any form of contact. I think she thought was I was gunna go mental in the house and shag anything moved like I had on *Ex on the Beach*. But I said to her that *Celebrity Big Brother* was different to those shows I had done and was a chance to show the nation that I was more than a tongue-flapping fanny bandit. Francesca was sound, and to give her credit she said to me, 'Scott, I wouldn't stop you doing anything. Just do one thing for me – go into that house and WIN!!'

Having Francesca give me the seal of approval was what

I needed to hear. Before I left for *Celebrity Big Brother*, I slipped a letter into her bag telling her that I loved her and that I wanted to marry her. It was how I was feeling and I needed to share me feelings with her.

A couple of days after new year and a day or two before the *Celebrity Big Brother* launch night, I had to film the profile shoots that they show just before the celebrities go into the house. I arrived at a bar called Love & Liquor in north London where Hannah, one of the producers, greeted me with a kiss.

Over the next five hours I answered a bunch of questions about why I wanted to be on the show. 'I've been on *Geordie Shore* for ages and it's the same fucking people every day,' I said. 'I wake up and there's Charlotte hanging, stinking and I'd like to wake up to some new birds I can crack on to.' I even whipped off me shirt to flash me pecs and got down and did a set of press ups.

Then I recorded an interview with Christopher Biggins for the spin-off show *Big Brother's Bit on the Side*, which was hilarious. I heard afterwards that the crew was in hysterics while they were filming me – which was good to hear – and that the cameraman had found it hard to keep his camera still from laughing! Buzzing! Job boxed off.

Unlike classic *Big Brother*, the celeb contestants don't have to live in hiding for a week. Instead, we are held captive for just 36 hours in a hotel near the studios in Elstree. A car was sent to pick me up and I was driven out to Borehamwood. On the way, I asked the driver to cheekily stop off at some shops cos I suddenly thought to meself that I hadn't packed enough clothes. After about an hour, I finally got to the hotel where I was met by me own personal *CBB* chaperone called Liam Hatter, who was also a runner on *Geordie Shore*, and would stay with me in me cramped room for the next 36 hours. I was buzzing, though – cos I knew Liam already, it was chilled.

After about five minutes I was already climbing the walls. But I wasn't allowed to go anywhere, which is probably a good thing cos if they let me out I'd probably have went fucking aka, done a runner to a bar, got smashed out me skull and banged the barman. Hannah popped by again and went through the rules of the show and asked me if I had any last-minute requests.

'Could I get a spray tan and can we get me hairdresser down to London to give me a fade?' I asked.

Hannah laughed. 'We can't get you a tan, but I'm sure we can get one of our very talented hair and make up team to sort you out. Anything else?'

I thought long and hard, then said, 'Er, just Nandos, kid.'

And so that was that. I was milking it. Luckily, I had a series of press interviews lined up that day that most definitely helped break the monotony of being in that ill hotel room.

Next day was launch night and I couldn't wait to get going. Anything to get out of this fucking room! Even though I had heard rumours about who was going into the show (*TOWIE*'s Gemma Collins and Megan McKenna), the producers kept us all apart so we didn't lay eyes on each other until we went into the house, cos if I'd have crossed paths with them I'd have probs tried to dust Megan.

I decided to wear a crisp white shirt and jeans for me going in outfit. I was gunna wear a belt that I had bought the day before but producers told me last minute I couldn't take it in cos it had a logo on it that would break some kind of advertising rule. The bastards – that belt cost a fucking fortune, Louis Vuitton badboy!

When it was me call time, I was raring to go. Liam and I jumped in a car and I was driven to the studio and waited for me turn to be introduced. As I sat in the car I could hear the sound of the audience cheering and screaming. There was a real buzz in the air, like, and I couldn't wait to in the mix.

Just before Emma Willis announced me on stage, I was taken up to stand behind the 'Eye' door that we step through and was greeted by two fit lasses standing on either side of me wearing these sexy burlesque basques. Then Emma called me name and I jumped through the eye and bounced down the catwalk. Oi, oi, that Emma's a fittie. Matt Willis, you are a lucky man, kid!

The audience was wild and sounded like they were fucking crackers. But they seemed to like a bit of turbo so I was pleased! After a quick chat about me love of birds and me nan, Emma sent me on me way and I finally stepped into the *CBB* house.

As I bounced down the stairs the first two people I saw were Megan, who looked fucking lethal, and Gemma Collins, whose hair was so big she looked like fucking Aslan from *The Lion, the Witch and the Wardrobe*. Then I said me hellos to David Gest, Daniella Westbrook from *EastEnders*,

Christopher Maloney, that rascal from *The X Factor*, and Tiffany Pollard, a sound black woman with drag queen hair and tits so big, they looked like a couple of space hoppers. I had never seen her in anything, but understood she was a massive reality TV star in the US. I could tell she was gunna be a lot of fun and would be TV gold.

For the next hour or so the rest of the housemates came in one by one, including, *Strictly*'s Kristina Rihanoff, who would announce in the house she was pregnant, Kim Kardashian's mate Jonathan Cheban, ex-*EastEnders* star John Partridge, star of the musicals and former lothario Darren Day, David Bowie's ex-wife Angie, model and heavily tattooed reality star Jeremy McConnell and ex-*Hollyoaks* actress Steph Davis and even fucking Winston McKenzie. Once everyone was in and settled, we popped open some booze and got to know each other. Everyone seemed to be a laugh to be honest – easy to say on the first night – but there were some really big characters, so it was gunna be interesting to see how we all got on as the weeks progressed and who would end up ripping each other's heeds off.

To begin with, I forged a close relationship with Megan, Steph and Jeremy – probably cos we were all around the same age and looked like we were up for fun. Jeremy was a lovely bloke, a real nice gentleman who told us about how he had lost his mam and brother and sister and carried their pictures around with him in a locket. He was a good-looking guy with a lot on his mind. I liked him from the off. Steph seemed sound too. She told me she had been fired from *Hollyoaks* for turning up to work late after boozy nights out on the piss, so I guessed we had a lot in common. She also spent the first day or two gushing on about her boyfriend Sam Reece. And Megan, well, we knew each other from *Ex on the Beach*.

It didn't take long for me to realise that being in that house was actually quite boring. Don't forget you see just 42 minutes of a 24-hour day. Most of the time we'd sit on the sofas or out in the smoking area just chatting shit, mainly about what we were doing in our work lives.

Honestly, there is nothing to do in that house. And when there are so many people crammed into such a small space it can be quite overwhelming. There's no escaping the endless chatter unless you go for a shit or speak to Big Brother in the diary room.

Every so often Big Brother would give us tasks to do, which helped ease the boredom, although they tended to dissolve into massive kick-offs. One of me favourite tasks was the ventriloquist one where 'puppet masters' and 'puppets' would be forced to answer some awkward questions about their housemates or perform a task. When the puppets were forced to swallow a rotten egg, I nearly pissed meself. Megan puked in her box and Christopher spent about half an hour gagging, though I thought he'd be used to that. It was so funny.

Although not a task, the day that Tiffany thought David Gest was dead had us cracking up too (it was gutting to hear of his death a few months later). If you didn't see it, YouTube it – it's TV gold. Angie Bowie had just been told that her ex-husband David had died from cancer. Still in shock and feeling upset, Angie confided in Tiffany about the sad news.

Only Tiffany thought that Angie was talking about David Gest who had been pretty poorly during his stay in the house and started screaming and hollering. I guess if you had heard the words 'David is dead', you'd be bound to think 'What? David? The man we've been sharing the house with who has been sick?' So I could understand her initial reaction. But when she found out about the confusion and that David was actually alive it all kicked off, with Tiffany having a go at Angie, Jonny hating Tiffany and then Megan kicking off at John. It got noisy and I just stepped away me, like!

When we weren't doing tasks, everyone seemed to be fighting with each other. Megan had a real beef against John cos she thought he was a sneak, plus the fact that she had about 19 screws loose. But many of her arguments kicked off after she'd had a few drinks and got carried away with herself.

Megan's actually a good girl, even though she had massive meltdowns in the house. Away from the cameras she's nice but when she's 'on' I dunno how to take her. I think she shouldn't get involved in anything to do with telly if I'm honest. Cos we knew each other from before, we were pretty close and felt comfortable enough to hug – we even had a cheeky neck at one point, but it meant nothing, I didn't even fancy her, but I think we just did it cos we were bored and I was thinking with me choppa.

For the record, I really liked Jonny Cheban. He was an outspoken guy for sure but he was lovely to me. He was honest and he loved getting stuck in to those arguments, winding people up! But Jonny and I share a very special bond. I actually owe him me life! There was one day in the house we were sitting around having dinner. I took a mouthful of steak and suddenly I felt it wedge in me throat. I tried to cough it up but it wouldn't budge. I tried a gulp of water to dislodge it but it just wouldn't shift. In fact it made me choke more. I started to panic and then turned blue and collapsed. Luckily Jonny jumped up, grabbed me from behind, did the Heimlich manoeuvre and it popped out and I was saved. I genuinely thought I was gunna die and I'm guessing the sight of me turning blue was fucking lifting for *Celebrity Big Brother* to screen.

As Stephanie and Jeremy got closer and it became clear that their relationship was more than just friendship, the rest of us started to feel uncomfortable. I mean, what they were doing didn't affect us directly, but we couldn't help wonder what her poor boyfriend must be thinking at home. I tried me best to advise Jeremy to step back but he didn't listen – in one ear and out his fucking arsehole. When Steph heard that, she got pissed off with me for sticking me nose in.

Their relationship was really pissing me off – I wanted to hang out with Jeremy cos I thought he was sound, but I could see him losing himself cos she was so controlling. I could see right through it.

I just didn't get Steph in the end. She had come in telling everyone she planned to marry this guy Sam and then blatantly made a play for Jeremy. I tried to warn Jez that if she's done it here, she'll do it again. But he wouldn't listen.

And don't get me started on all the stuff they have done since the show – that really pissed me off too. It was all so attention-seeking. I know it's good to be in the media and be written about if that's your job, but what is she doing? Breaking up and arguing in public was bad enough, but announcing she was pregnant online was just one step too far! It's, like, what the fuck? What are you doing? Why are you doing this in public? Have you got any dignity, kid? I just think it makes them look stupid. I haven't seen Steph since the show. I speak to Jeremy from time to time but I don't tell him what to do any more – I can't be arsed. He has to make his own mistakes.

Talking of attention seekers, Gemma Collins was probably the worst, but I think it's just who she is. I had actually never met her before this and she was just as loud and as brash as I expected her to be, but she was fucking funny. There were a few occasions when she and Daniella would storm off in a huff and threaten to leave, but no one cared; it was all for attention. She cracked me up though. One day she kicked off during a game when half of us were in the task room. The people in the living room were shown a picture of someone in the task room and we had to guess who it was by asking questions. So we had to ask questions like, 'Is she lazy?' and someone asked 'Is it Gemma?' She protested that she wasn't lazy at all. Then the very next day we had a spinning class and she didn't get out of bed, the radgie.

Tiffany proved me right and turned out to be a pretty radge lass. She was very sexual and was always talking about sex and stuff. She was just like a girl version of me. We necked on a few times but it was all just a bit of fun. She seemed obsessed with me and me cock. There was one time

I was in the shower and she came to look at me goods and said: 'WOW, that's nice. I can see what you're working with. That's huge, that could blow me back out!' See, a girl just like me!

Of all the people in the house Darren was me favourite. I just really warmed to him. I mean, he's been through a lot. He's had a mental life and he told me some wild stories, like when he was a bad womaniser and got up to all sorts. He sounded a bit like me and I could relate to many of the stories he was telling. I can just imagine them happening to me. He's such a funny bloke. He has kids now so he's settled down a lot and is living a really happy life. I have a feeling that one day I am gunna be just like him, after I've got all the wildness out me system.

Then, yeah, I won. I won the fucking show!

He has a heart of gold and was so lovely in that house, I really wanted him to win. I felt honoured to meet someone like him and I have such great respect for him. And I'm so pleased he was in the final with me and came out of the show with people seeing a different side to him. And he was so happy for me to win.

Then, yeah, I won. I won the fucking show, man! Scotty Turbo T! I couldn't believe it. I really couldn't. But then I also couldn't believe that Stephanie of all people was runner up. When me name was called by Emma, I felt on top of the world. I'd come into this experience to show people another side of meself and I think I had. I was not just the lairy shagger people had seen on *Geordie Shore*. I showed them that

I could be sensitive and serious Scotty too – well, even if I did tell all me housemates about the time I shit meself when I was shagging that bird.

When the doors opened and I emerged as the winner, I could barely hear meself think as the crowds below screamed their hearts out. I couldn't believe this was happening to me. It meant that people had been voting for me cos they liked us. I glided down the stairs as if I was floating, greeted Emma Willis with a big hug and then pouted for the paps. After the winner's interview with Emma, I was whisked off to meet Rylan on *BBBOTS*, but as I had a wee bit of time, I quickly called Francesca to see if she was okay …

She was over the moon that I had won and told me she was so proud of me (good, so me innocent snogs hadn't pissed her off that much – even though we weren't officially together I thought she'd be a bit annoyed). I was really overwhelmed by the whole situation and I couldn't wait to see her and make up for lost time.

Unfortunately, before I could, I was back on *Geordie Shore* to film something for the birthday episode. But we did get to hook up on Valentine's Day where I finally caught up with her and took her out for dinner. As I looked into her eyes and toasted our night, I couldn't help but think that life really couldn't get any better.

30

THE FUTURE

Winning *Celebrity Big Brother* didn't change me but it really changed me life. No sooner was I back in the real world than I was being offered all sorts. Fashion label Boohoo invited me to become the face of their menswear collection. Me? A model? Who'd have thought it, eh? But it's been a hell of a lot of fun and the people who own the company are an amazing family and have really looked after me.

Although I was used to doing promo shoots for the TV shows and shoots for magazines, I found out that modelling is a lot different cos it's not just about you; you have to showcase the clothes in the best way possible. Even though I wouldn't say I was vain, I am so conscious about the way I look, especially me hair, that I must have driven the styling team mad on the shoots. But I gave the best blue steel I could and everyone seemed buzzing!

Meanwhile, male strip troop The Dream Boys asked me to

join them on their tour, which meant that I finally got me Magic Mike Moment, flapping me cock about on stage. I was nervous about it to start with cos first of all the rest of the Dream Boys have amazing bodies, and I needed to get toned up after three weeks in the *Big Brother* house. I was also concerned about the choreography that went with the performance. I can dance but I'd have to learn a routine. That was hard but I nailed it! And then of course I was worried about the stripping itself. Luckily, I was reassured to find out that I only had to strip down to me underwear! I'm not allowed to get me full choppa out in case people take pictures of me and send them to the papers!

I met all the lads and they were sound and when I did me first few shows, the screams from the crowd really help you get going. I'm only on for about ten minutes but I come out wearing a mask then take it off and the place goes fucking mad. Francesca came to one of the shows and queued up after the show to get a picture signed! She said she was very impressed with what she saw.

Another highlight was getting to shoot a cameo role in Aussie soap *Neighbours*. Cos I'm so popular in Australia the producers asked me to film a scene for the show. Basically, I am jogging around Lassiter's and bump into Aaron Brennan, played by Matt Wilson, and we have this crazy conversation where we don't understand what either of us are saying. To be honest, on set I don't think people understood a word I was saying anyway! But it was great fun. I was a bit anxious when I turned up on set cos I hadn't acted before (aside from that Basshunter video!). But everyone on the team made me

271

feel great and now they want me to come back and do another scene. So, exciting times ahead.

Now, just in case you think I've turned over a new leaf and left me bad boy ways behind, don't be silly, I'm still a fucking absolute radge packet! Back in May, I did something really stupid. I had just got back to Newcastle from a bunch of PAs and me mate came to pick me up from the station. On the way home, we pulled up to the chippy in Heaton where me other mate lived and I went to put me bag in the boot. In the boot me mate had an air rifle so I grabbed it and started playing around with it – just like I did when I was a kid. And you know what I'm like when I get giddy, I just get carried away. So I said to me mate, 'Get a photo of me looking like a sniper!'

And me mate said, 'Go on, get on top of the car!'

So I did and then posted the picture on Twitter and said something about being 'Scotty sniper patrolling the city on Neighbourhood Watch!', and then didn't think anything more about it.

Then, about 40 minutes later, there were some dodgy comments and I started to think perhaps I might actually get in trouble. But I still didn't think of the severity of it.

But then the police got in touch and I thought, 'Oh shit!'

The police said they wanted to speak to me, so they took me into the station and detained me while they searched me house. When they found nothing, they cautioned me.

Yes, I have learnt me lesson. Well, until the next time anyway.

*

I'm sticking with *Geordie Shore* for the foreseeable future, but let's see what happens – who knows what is around the corner? I love being on the show and I love the people, so I am in no rush to go anywhere. But I would like to do some more acting. If Jason Statham can make it in Hollywood, why can't Scotty T, like?!

And what's happening with Francesca? At the time of writing, I'd say we're just going with the flow. She's a good laugh. The thing is, I couldn't do what I did on the show if I wasn't single. I wouldn't be where I am now. As I said, people watch the show cos they like the fun side of me. They see all the others in relationships and they see me just have a laugh, cos I don't give a fuck and I'm always after a shag.

Even though I really like Francesca and can imagine meself with her for a long time, *Geordie Shore* is me bread and butter. I need to make enough money to set meself up for the future. So I am not gunna sacrifice it right now, but in the forseeable future, who knows? It could be no more pulling for me.

At the start we were quite casual, so she didn't mind us getting with girls on the show but we've got closer and closer over time and she has started to get upset. And it upsets me too as she's literally the best lass. I can go out clubbing with her and enjoy meself which I have never been able to do with a previous girlfriend. She's mint. She's class. She doesn't try to change me but keeps me grounded and stops me going AWOL. She has been so supportive. She's amazing. I would love to marry her one day. But I can't right now cos I have to do this work and make lots of money.

I really think I have found the one and I know she'll stick by me. And she's just right for me cos she is everything you could want in a girl. She's an honest girl, the most honest girl I know. She is a special girl and I try to make her feel as special as I can. I take her to nice places, I get her gifts, and we have a propa fucking laugh together, not to mention she's got the best arse in the land.

Most importantly, me mam loves her, and she's the only girl I have properly introduced to me nan! And I like to think that up there somewhere me granddad thinks I've found meself a pure mint girl, just like he did with me nan!

But I'm always gunna be the same Scotty T, so make sure to catch up on the next edition, cos there's so much more that people need to know (there's only so many pages and what with me concentration span, I can't even remember what I've written in here). But I hope you enjoyed it, you bunch of radgies. See you in a bit. What a fucking great book!

ACKNOWLEDGEMENTS

Well, firstly I think it's only fair that I thank Mam and Dad. Without them I wouldn't exist. I have to give them credit for putting up with me being an absolute nightmare, like. Mam and Dad, you are fucking soldiers, but look at how great I turned out to be!

To me loving grandparents on both sides, for being so supportive, especially Granddad Richard, who I know is looking down on me with a big grin on his face.

To me extended family: Carol, for keeping me in line, and Jamie for teaching me the Force (with me choppa) and making me the confident Scotty T you see before you today.

To the boys, I love each and every one of you daft cunts to bits – we've been through it all, and I know we'll be friends for life.

To everyone who has been mentioned in the book, from all of you on the club and bar scene, and me castmates in *Geordie Shore*, *Ex on the Beach* and *Celebrity Big Brother*. I can't do a shout out to you all but know that if I have your number, I love ya.

To all me previous girlfriends, you are all rascals. Fair play to you all, and you know we had a laugh, even with me Scotty T ways. And to Fran, you know how I feel.

To K, and all the team at BLVK, especially Adam, who have worked non-stop to allow me to keep acting radge 24/7. Massive thanks also to the people who gave me this opportunity – Steve Regan, Kerry Taylor, Craig Orr and Jake Atwell, as well as all the press team at MTV and Lime Pictures. I fucking love you all.

And before I forget, to the entire team at Simon & Schuster for publishing me book. Big kisses to me editor, Nicki Crossley; without her this book would never have seen the light of day. Sorry to the copy-editor who had to correct me grammar! I know I'm a pain in the arse but I'm so happy with what you have helped me create.

And huge thanks to David Riding; this is the second project he has worked on with me team and he worked fucking hard to make this happen. Thank you.

At the end of the day, I've lived life to the max and had a radge time so far. I know I have drama, but I hope you all know me heart is the right place. I hope you enjoyed this book, and I look forward to you all reading the next instalment…

Much love,

Scott X

PICTURE CREDITS

Page 1: Author's own

Page 2: Author's own

Page 3: Author's own

Page 4: All photos © Lime Pictures

Page 5: Author's own

Page 6: Top; author's own, middle right; © Getty Images, middle left and bottom; author's own

Page 7: Top; author's own, middle left and right; © Getty Images, bottom; author's own

Page 8: Author's own